WASHI CRAFTS

Working with Japanese Handmade Paper

Andrea Heinrichsohn

Shufunotomo Co., Ltd.

To my father,
who taught me to have the courage to go ahead and make dreams come true

Photography: Hitoshi Umezawa, Teddy Heinrichsohn
Book Design: Momoyo Nishimura

First Printing, 1999

Published by
Shufunotomo Co., Ltd.
2-9 Kanda Surugadai, Chiyoda-ku, Tokyo
101-8911 Japan

Printed in Hong Kong

ISBN 4-07-976340-9

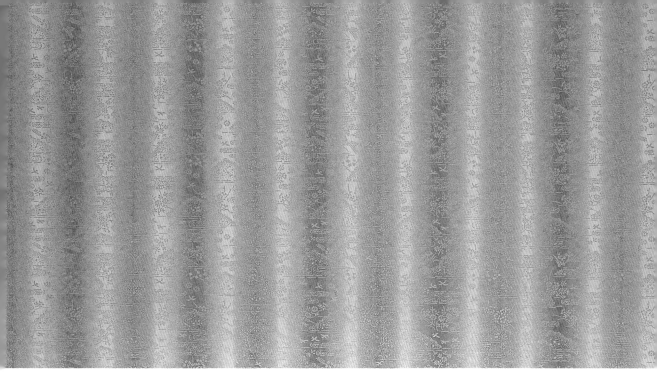

CONTENTS

Acknowledgements

This book is the result of several lucky factors. I consider myself lucky, for example, to have learned from my very pragmatic father, Mr. William Nichol, not to join the hordes of those who say, "If I had had the chance, I would have..." or "I wish I had done such and such." This teaching encouraged me to learn to fly, an achievement I look back on with pride and great pleasure. He taught me that if I really wanted to do something, I should get up and do what was necessary to make it happen. Publishing this book is my way of saying thank you. I hope to be able to enrich the lives of my children, Peter and Kandy, by passing on my father's teaching.

I have enjoyed the beauty of *washi*, or Japanese handmade paper in general, for eight years and thought about whether to write this book for all of three. For quite some time I wondered whether I would ever manage to really have my book published in this very foreign land, not knowing where to start. A very dear friend of over 30 years, Mr. Musashi Kawasaki, encouraged and helped me. Without his guidance I would surely have made one blunder after the other and perhaps not have succeeded. Also, Mr. Saburo Nobuki, President of the International Publishing Institute, guided and helped me with a firm hand and a gentle heart. Despite delays and disappointments, he persevered. A very good friend, Mrs. Inge Niehaus, encouraged me to write. She believed in my ability to express myself and said so. In the final weeks, another good friend, Mrs. Eva-Maria Juras, helped me selflessly with practical advice. I am most indebted to her. Mrs. Isabelle Haessler lent me her entire home to take the photographs shown in this book. Without her paintings and antiques, it would have been impossible to show the items in such a lovely setting. Having Miss Kimberly Scott as my editor was a little like winning the lottery. She is gentle, understanding and a true professional. And finally my husband, Teddy Heinrichsohn, master minded the technical photographs that I hope will help you to follow the instructions in this book. When I should have been helping to unpack over a thousand boxes after our move from Japan to Germany, he took on most of the work and did all the cooking to leave me the time I needed to meet my deadline.

One of the attractions of writing this book, apart from the obvious desire to share the beauty of washi and the making of washi eggs and crafts with others, has been the notion that washi eggs combine the beauty of Japanese handmade paper and the Western custom of decorating eggs which goes back hundreds of years. The much talked about, but seldom realized, dream of internationalization comes alive in the simple and beautiful craft of washi egg making.

I wish you luck and much pleasure as you go on to make your own washi egg treasures and other washi crafts.

Andrea Heinrichsohn

Introduction

I first became acquainted with Japanese handmade paper while living in Europe. A Japanese friend brought me a present wrapped beautifully in thick purple and grey washi. The gift looked so noble I was reluctant to open it.

Once in Japan, I was stunned by the texture, variety and beauty of the washi I found there. I was excited and keen to use washi in my personal life but not quite sure how to go about it. A friend invited me to her home where she was giving a class in washi egg covering. In no time the afternoon had flown by, and even those among us who had said they were never very good at making things with their hands left with two or three almost finished eggs and big smiles. The moment I held one of her lovely eggs in the palm of my hand, I was reminded of the silky, sensuous feel of a *netsuke* and I fell in love with the beauty and luminosity of washi, its endless varieties, subtle shades and ever differing textures.

Once I had learned the basic art of covering eggs with washi, I started to experiment with different paper, egg sizes and decorative uses. I have taught people in small groups at home and the students have come from such diverse backgrounds as potter, medical doctor and housewife. I remember one lady to whom I showed the basic steps of making washi eggs while our husbands were discussing business matters. Two days later she phoned to tell me she had gone out the very next day and had bought washi and lacquer and then worked until one in the morning, unable to put her "works of art" aside. That she had forgotten to spoon her eggs – and that they were therefore rather bumpy – in no way detracted from her excitement. Today she lives in Germany and holds classes on washi egg covering at a health resort.

One of the most amazing stories I have experienced among those I have introduced to this art concerns another German lady. We have since become good friends. She is a designer, dress maker and book binder by trade. She came to stay with me for a short visit and as we chatted, I made a few eggs. She watched, was fascinated, and took some washi home with her. She now sells her eggs to private individuals, to boutiques, and at exhibitions she arranges at home. She has even had an order from Peru for twenty eggs of a certain color. This Easter she sold her eggs and donated the money to a group of German doctors who travel to war ravaged countries to operate on children who are victims of war. The money from her eggs this year made it possible for two children to be operated on.

Another interesting experience was when I was invited to Nagoya to teach the art of washi egg making to a group of Japanese ladies who were then to teach elderly people living in a home for the aged. Washi eggs are quite inexpensive to make, and are lovely, personal gifts which I hoped would bring pleasure to the elderly in the home we visited.

But it is perhaps my own experience of pride and pleasure when visitors to my home admire my eggs that is the most rewarding. Friends to whom I have given an egg for a particular occasion are touched and it feels good to be able to bring pleasure with something as small and simple as a washi egg. My eggs have even been on television. This moment of fame came about when my husband was being interviewed by a popular television personality who noticed a bowl of washi eggs on my sitting room table. To my great amusement, she stopped abruptly and admired each egg, asking detailed questions about how and of what they were made.

The beauty of washi still fascinates me many years after my first encounter with it in Germany, and although I still love making washi eggs, it was a logical step to look for new ways to enjoy its beauty. I covered tea boxes of all sizes and they are lovely but there really is a limit to how many covered tea boxes one can use in a home. I wanted to be able to incorporate washi into my everyday life and step by step I added the practical crafts you will find in Part II of this book to my repertoire. I have included objects that are easy to make as well as more challenging projects that you can enjoy making for your own home or as pretty gifts for friends. Whether you decide to make a candle shade for your tea table or something more ambitious such as the lovely album on page 74, I hope you will enjoy working with me and that you will be inspired to explore the many ways to enjoy this beautiful craft on your own.

The strength, beauty and permanence of washi is due largely to the gentle handling of the fibers throughout the papermaking process. Washi is made in many thicknesses. There are thin white sheets that look just like lace, medium thick sheets that have a shiny surface, thick sheets that have a lovely, naturally rough surface, and the most common kind which is about as thick as good writing paper but much more supple. Whereas an egg can be covered in all but the thickest kind, the latter one is the easiest to work with and comes in the greatest variety of patterns.

Speaking of patterns, there are hundreds to choose from and new designs are brought out every year. Some are bold and depict the dramatic faces of kabuki actors, for example; others are pale shades of lilac and pink with gold dust sprinkled all over. Flowers of all sizes and butterflies seem to be the favorites. I have never seen a washi pattern that I have not liked. By the time the paper is lacquered, the colors positively radiate.

I have tried to write a handicraft book that can really be followed, that holds nothing back. So often we buy a book, only to discover that it describes the obvious and leaves out the secrets. The art of making washi eggs – my personal passion and the impetus for the creation of this book – merits an entire section to itself. The crafts in Part II are listed in order of difficulty. I suggest you read through each chapter before you begin, and pay special attention to the tip boxes found throughout the book.

Getting Started: Notes on Materials

I suggest you read through the following description of materials you will need before you allow your enthusiasm to run away with you. For those of you who live in Japan, I have provided the Japanese in italics. This will be helpful when you are faced with the task of explaining to the charming salesperson behind the counter that you are looking for lacquer!

Glue (*bondo*)
Any strong household glue will work well with these crafts.

Japanese Handmade Paper (*washi*)
Washi is most commonly available in the following approximate dimensions:

Full sheet	25 1/2" x 38" (65cm X 97cm)
1/2 sheet	12 1/2" x 38" (32cm X 97cm)
1/3 sheet	12 1/2" x 24 3/4" (32cm X 63cm)
1/4 sheet	12 1/2" x 19 1/4" (32cm X 49cm)
Squares	6" x 6" (15cm X 15cm)

In Japan there are many shops specializing in washi, but in other countries try looking for it in well-stocked stationers, gift shops and shops selling items made from handmade paper. See "Washi Sources" on page 95 for a sampling of shops throughout the world which stock washi.

Lacquer (*suyadashi-eki*)
For washi eggs and smaller crafts, I recommend applying the lacquer with a brush. Make sure that the lacquer you buy dries with a clear finish and that the brush can be washed in water. A product with a brush fitted into its lid has the advantage that the brush remains in the lacquer and does not need to be cleaned. When using lacquer, it is best to be careful to either keep the brush in the lacquer when not in use or wash it out after each use. This is because lacquer dries like crumbs and if you were to use the brush without either keeping it away from the air or washing it, you would brush the crumbs onto the surface of your egg or craft. Spray-on lacquers may be used with the larger crafts.

Paste (*nori*)
When shopping for paste, make sure that the type you purchase dries slowly. I recommend a slow-drying paste so that you don't need to worry if you don't lay the washi in exactly the right place the first time. Some craft shops sell small packets of powdered paste which must be mixed with water before use. Paste that is recommended for wall papering can also be used. Most probably any prepared paste will be too thick, therefore you will have to dilute it with water to the consistency of thick, but still runny, honey. Mix the paste well to ensure there are no lumps, and avoid using too much.

Pumping Device for Egg - Optional
There is an easy-to-use, easy-to-clean device for removing the contents from an egg called Blas-Fix®. If it isn't available in a handicraft shop in your town, you might like to write to the makers and ask how you can obtain one: Johannes Zemlin GmbH, 2,000 Hamburg 54, Germany. The product number is 001027.

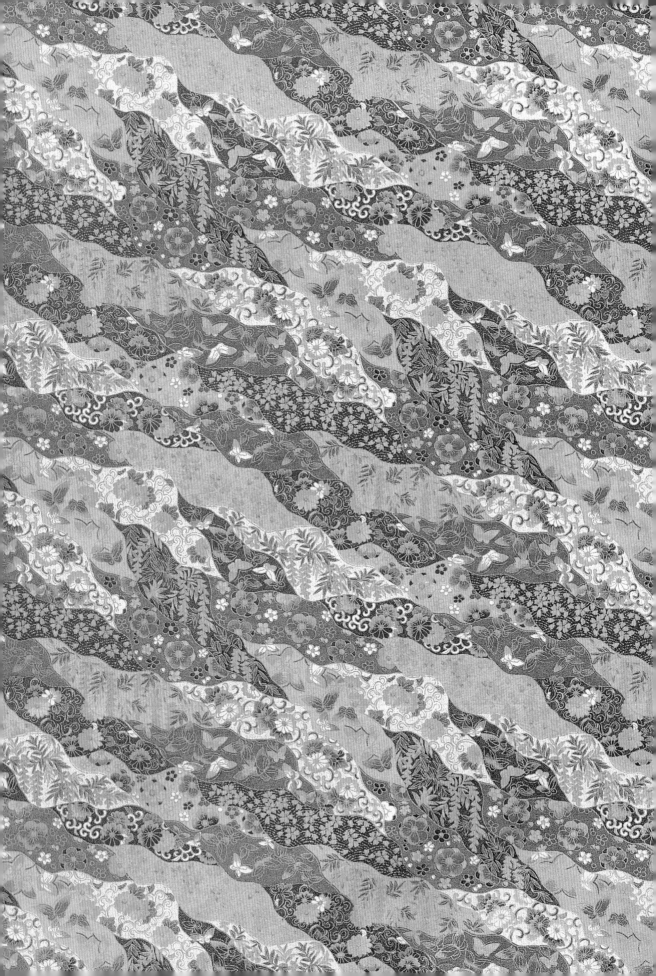

Part I

The Art of Washi Egg Making

Washi Eggs

MATERIALS
Egg at room temperature
Well-sharpened, medium-soft pencil
Pin or other sharp object to make holes
   in egg
Cake tester
Soft tape measure
Short ruler
Square piece of washi paper
   approximately 6" x 6" (15cm x 15cm)
Pair of sharp, small scissors
   that you can hold comfortably
Paste
Container for paste,
   preferably with well-fitting lid
Brush, approximately 3/4" (2cm) wide –
   optional
Bottle of lacquer
Small, medium-soft brush for lacquer
Soup spoon
Old newspaper
Damp cloth

When you accept an invitation to dinner or to tea, a washi egg is a delightful way of thanking your hostess for her kind invitation and is a lovely alternative to flowers.

12

I. Prepare the Egg

It is a good idea to make it a habit throughout the year to blow an egg each time you use one in the kitchen so that you have a ready supply on hand. Brown-shelled eggs are fine unless the washi you are working with is white or pastel. Before you begin, file any hard specks on the egg smooth with an emery board.

1. Hold the egg upright, at eye level, and make a pencil mark at the center of one end. Rotate the egg a quarter of a turn and make another mark. Choose a point between the two and make another mark. That will be the center point. Do the same in the other end.

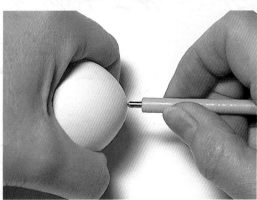

2. Using a pin or other sharp object, make holes at the center of each end. You can keep the hole through which you will be blowing fairly small, and make the hole at the other end a little larger by carefully chipping off minute pieces from the edge.

3. Using a long needle or cake tester, break up the yolk by poking around inside the egg. Blow gently through one hole until the egg is empty, and rinse the inside of the egg thoroughly with water. Prop the egg up and allow to dry for 24 hours.

To be sure that no yolk or egg white remains in the egg, fill the egg with water, hold both holes shut, shake the egg and again blow out the contents. When filling the egg, it helps to keep the cake tester in the egg to keep the hole open.

II. Measure the Length and Breadth of the Egg

Choose a table near the window or at least a place which is well lit. If you are making your first washi egg, I suggest you choose paper that has a small, uniform pattern with no one element dominating. If you are the adventurous type or have tried your hand at washi eggs before, the following is worth considering: In order to keep a large motif in its entirety, you will probably have to adjust the top edge of your washi as you measure the egg so that your chosen motif is placed around the fattest part of the egg. Patterns with large elements are a little more difficult to handle than a more uniform spray of tiny flowers, but they are well worth the trouble.

1. Measure the distance between the two holes using a soft tape measure. Be exact. As you learn which types of washi stretch when wet, you can subtract 1/16" (1-2mm) accordingly.

2. Place a ruler on the back of your piece of washi and, measuring from the edge of the paper, make a mark to show the length of the egg.

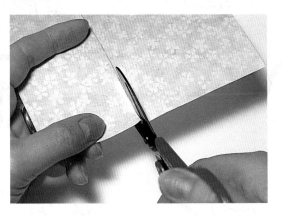

3. Draw a thin line across the paper at the height of the pencil mark and cut along the pencil line.

4. Wrap the paper around the egg and mark the spot where the ends meet at the thickest part of the egg with a pencil. Be exact. It is, however, better to have a little too much paper than too little!

5. Lay the egg to one side and, using your ruler, draw a vertical line through the pencil mark. Cut off the excess paper. Now fold the paper in half lengthwise, patterned side inside.

III. Draw a Pattern

1. Place the folded paper on your work surface with the fold at the top. Using your ruler, measure a point 5/16″ (8mm) down from the fold. (You may need to measure anywhere from 3/16″ [5mm] for a smallish or very rounded egg to 1/2″ [1-2cm] for a larger and longer egg.) For the sake of accuracy, make a mark at both ends of the folded paper.

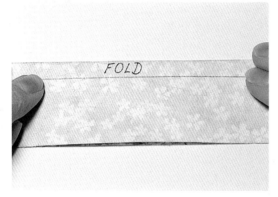

2. Draw a faint line across the paper. Take care not to press too hard, especially if you are using a pale colored washi, as it may show through to the patterned side.

If your washi has a large element that you hope to keep in one piece, lightly trace its outline onto the back of the washi before you draw the pattern. When you draw the vertical lines in step 6, you can widen or narrow the section involved.

If the vertical cut that you will soon be making along the pencil line must cut into a larger motif you hope to center on the egg, it is best to place the motif in such a way that only the last 1/4″ (4-5mm) of the cut disturb it. By the time the fringes have been placed and pasted and the egg has been spooned, you will hardly notice the cut.

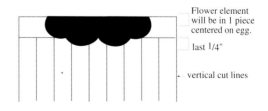

Flower element will be in 1 piece centered on egg.

last 1/4″

vertical cut lines

3. Measuring from the bottom edge upward, make a mark 3/4″ (18mm) from the lower edge. Again, do this at both sides.

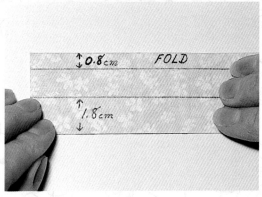

4. Using a ruler, draw a thin line right across the paper, joining the two marks.

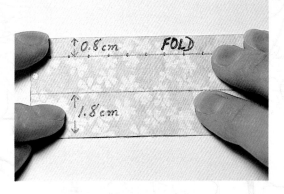

5. Now lay your ruler along the top pencil line. At intervals of 5/16″ (8mm) make small pencil marks all along the line.

6. Place the short end of the ruler flush against the line nearest the fold and draw a faint vertical line from each point along the upper line to the lower edge of your paper.

IV. Cut a Pattern

Method 1

1. Starting at the lower right edge of your paper if you are right handed, cut upwards from the center of the first oblong section to the top right hand corner of the same section.

2. Return to the exact point at which you started and cut upward to the top left corner of that section.

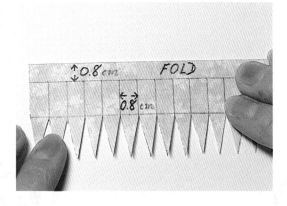

3. Repeat this step right across the paper, moving from right to left. The fringes are now clearly visible.

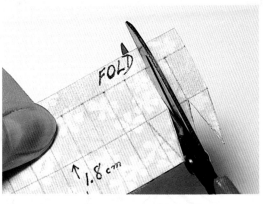

4. Now cut along the vertically drawn pencil lines as far as the top horizontal line on your paper.

Method 2

This method takes a little longer and requires a good eye and some experience in making washi eggs. The advantage is that you cut more paper from between the fringes which in turn means less overlap when you lay the fringes and finally, smoother seams. You can also adjust the width of each fringe to save an important part of a motif.

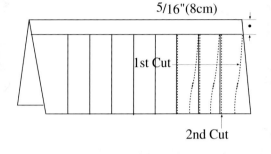

5/16"(8cm)

1st Cut

2nd Cut

1. Follow the directions for "Draw a Pattern" on page 17, except do not draw a line from the bottom.

2. Holding the folded paper in your left hand, (fold at the top), begin cutting from the right. Place your scissors at the bottom of the paper, in the middle of the last section on the right. As you begin cutting upwards, slowly curve your way outward, to the right, until by the last 1/3 of the section you are only cutting a sliver of paper.

3. Now cut straight up the vertical line.

4. Repeat these two cuts, moving from right to left, until all sections have been cut in this manner.

5. Turn the paper over and repeat the process described above, again moving from right to left

A Brief Word on the History of Papermaking

Papermaking began around AD 605 when T'sai Lun, a Chinese court official, developed the idea of forming a sheet of paper from the macerated bark of trees, hemp waste, old rags and fish nets. Japanese paper is made from the inner white bark, known as bast fibers, of either *kozo*, *mitsumata* or *gampi* trees. Kozo is closely related to the white and red mulberry trees common in North America. Every 100 kg of harvested tree produces only 5 kg of paper!

V. Wrap the Egg

Ideally, the short edges of the paper should meet around the middle of the egg, but you may find that your washi paper will stretch a little after you apply the paste and there may be some overlap, so cut off any excess paper. Be careful as any exposed shell can spoil the whole beauty of your finished washi egg.

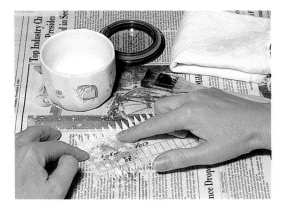

1. Open up the folded washi paper and place it, pattern side down, on top of your newspaper. Using either your finger or a brush 3/4" wide, spread the prepared paste all over the washi paper. Do this slowly, giving the paste a chance to be absorbed. Don't spread the paste too thickly. Wipe or brush off any excess paste.

2. Look at your pattern carefully to be sure the flowers are blooming the right way up, then place your egg horizontally on the short end of the washi and roll the egg in the washi.

3. Before you start to lay the fringes, check both ends to see if the tips of the fringes will meet, but be careful not to press the fringes onto the egg at this stage. If the egg is not centrally placed, move it either by squeezing it gently around the middle or, perhaps better still, rewrap it.

Lining your work surface with sheets of old newspaper makes it easy to clean up. Also, make sure you have a damp cloth close at hand; one of the secrets of a truly beautiful washi egg is having clean fingers and a clean working surface at all times.

VI. Lay the Fringes

1. Start to lay the fringes at one end, one by one, overlapping them slightly, until you have finished one end of the egg. If the tips dry while you are working, simply apply a little more paste with your finger.

2. If you measured accurately back at the beginning, the tips of the fringes should meet in a perfect point. But don't worry if they don't. The most practiced washi egg maker has trouble with this.

3. Before laying the fringes at the opposite end, check to see if the tips are going to meet or overlap. If they are too long, you can cut them at an angle to form new tips.

Sometimes after all the fringes have been laid you will notice that there is a small space or a pocket between and along the length of the fringes. If this is the case, it is a good idea to spread a thin layer of paste all over the outside of the egg making sure that the paste slips under the paper and into the pocket. Even if your finished egg is not perfect, don't worry. I will give you some tips later on how to cover up imperfections and to make your egg look just as lovely as you hope it will be.

VII. Smooth the Egg

1. Once you are satisfied that the fringes are as tidy as you can make them and before the egg dries, use the back of your thumb nail and the pads of your fingertips to smooth each seam and flatten any air bubbles. If you have used too much paste, now is the time to squeeze it out.

2. Lay your egg aside for an hour or so or until it is completely dry. This will be a good time to have a cup of tea or, less romantically, do what needs to be done.

VIII. Spoon the Egg

1. When it has dried well, hold the egg in the palm of your hand and, using the back of a soup spoon, smooth off the surface of your washi egg. You can apply quite a lot of pressure now and spoon along the seams and all over the egg until it feels completely smooth.

Easter Traditions

You may have wondered how Easter eggs came to be a part of the Easter tradition. It was in the 16th century, under the pressure of the reformation, that ancient seasonal rituals connected with the Spring equinox were gradually revived. Easter eggs were a popular part of these rituals as they were seen as symbols of new life and resurrection. There was a widespread belief that the sun danced for joy on Easter morning so people flocked to the hills at sunrise to see and take part in that wondrous event. Colored eggs were joyfully rolled down the slopes, red being the dominant color as it symbolized the blood of Christ.

IX. A Fun Step – Final Corrections

Missing Parts

Depending on the pattern of your washi, you have probably had to cut into a flower, shell or little figure. Try using a very fine, black, gold or silver felt pen to make up a missing petal or the tip of a tree. You can work wonders this way.

Sometimes it may be necessary, and easier, to correct a partly missing flower by cutting out the missing part from a remnant of the same washi pattern. Press the tiny replacement against the egg to check the fit and make any fine adjustments. Apply a little paste and press the replacement part firmly into place. Let it dry completely and spoon it as described in Step VIII.

Uneven Tips

Cut out a tiny flower from the scraps you have left over and place a blossom or a butterfly over the not quite perfect tips. This can prove to be so pretty that you may like to do it every time. It gives such a lovely finishing touch.

Egg Enhancement

By now, your washi egg is not the simple chicken egg you started with. Let it dry well before going on to complete your own personal treasure. No matter how many eggs you go on to create, each one becomes very special as you go along. This is the moment to add the date with a very fine brush or felt pen if the washi egg is to be given for a specific occasion such as the birth of a baby.

At one point in your washi egg making career you might like to try combining plain washi with a patterned one. The results can be quite unique. For instance, cover your egg in a plain colored washi. When it is dry and has been spooned, paste part of a pattern taken from a contrasting or matching colored washi in the desired position and dry and spoon again. You can then continue with the lacquering process as described above.

Another pretty idea you might like to experiment with is to dab or spread glitter (*kirari-nori*) over parts of your egg. Use the type which is mixed into a transparent paste and comes in small, plastic tubes. All you have to do is to squeeze a little onto your finger and dab or spread it, very sparingly, on parts of your not yet lacquered egg where you think it might enhance your work. It really looks very pretty on pale-colored washi. I recommend you try gold or silver at first.

A very sweet effect can be achieved by cutting out a butterfly and bending it slightly to imply flight. Lacquer it several times in that position. This will harden it. Finally, perch your butterfly on top of your egg using a tiny drop of strong glue to secure it. This can be done before or after you lacquer.

25

X. The Process of Lacquering

Don't be in a hurry with this phase! Some people simply use their fingers to lacquer their eggs, but it has been my experience that such eggs never achieve that lovely, silky touch that makes a washi egg such a delight to hold in your hand while admiring it. Watch for tiny bubbles that sometimes form in the lacquer while brushing. If they appear, simply brush them away.

1. Hold the bottom half of the egg in one hand and lacquer the surface of the egg that is visible. That will be approximately half of the egg. Be sure to lacquer very thinly. Brush off any excess lacquer. Stand the egg on its non-lacquered end in a small curtain ring or egg cup.

2. When it is dry, turn it around and lacquer the other half. In total, you should give your egg 6 to 8 layers of lacquer. The first two coats can be applied within a couple of hours of each other. After that, apply two half-coats a day for about four or five days. That makes one complete coat a day.

If the climate where you live is very dry, lacquering two half coats a day is fine, but in a damp climate it might be better to be even more patient and give your egg just one half coat a day.

XI. Sanding the Finished Egg – Optional

This next step will warm the hearts of the perfectionists among you. All you will need is a small piece of fine sandpaper to improve any minor faults that may have occurred, despite all efforts to the contrary. When purchasing sandpaper, it is important to know that the number indicates the degree of roughness; the higher the number, the finer the sandpaper. The sandpaper you will need feels almost as smooth as silk. Make sure the sandpaper you buy is meant to be used dry.

1. Using a 6" x 6" (15cm x 15cm) square of #600 sandpaper, gently file away the protruding layers of lacquer above the ridge or burst air bubble. (The clever device seen in the photo is a sandpaper holder.)

2. When you have sandpapered your washi egg to absolute perfection, simply lacquer your egg with one final coat. It is beautiful, isn't it?

When you first try this sandpapering technique, you will notice the lacquer turning cloudy. Please don't worry! I almost panicked when I first did it but no sooner had I re-lacquered my egg, than the cloudiness disappeared as if by magic. Hundreds of years ago this technique was used by master craftsmen in Italy and France when making furniture for noblemen and kings, so don't be afraid to give it a try.

Storing Washi Eggs

Should you want to put your washi eggs away for a while or to send a few to a friend as a present, please make sure that they are wrapped individually in tissue paper. If they touch for any length of time, they tend to stick together. Again, the climate in your part of the world is an important factor here.

Once, I covered an egg in red washi and then added the label from a bottle of wine I had shared with a friend. The wine was made in the same year as her daughter was born and she seemed to enjoy the gift very much when I gave it to her a few weeks later.

If you experiment with ways to use washi eggs to decorate your home, I am sure you will find some lovely combinations. The long, slender fingers of this hand inspired me to use objects that incorporate complimentary parallel lines, as can be seen in the stone and the obi that I used as a mat.

Whether you are having friends over for an informal luncheon or are planning to entertain someone special, you will want your table to be both attractive and unique. Try placing a washi egg in front of each guest as a favor, or heap them in a pretty bowl in the center of the table flanked by smaller bowls of flowers. If you have a large table, scatter them at random over the table interspersed with flowers and tiny washi eggs made from quail eggs.

Placing a small group of washi eggs made in subtle tones on an antique side table may result in your never wanting to view the table in any other way.

Wrapping Washi Eggs as Gifts

Whether you are handing the washi egg to a friend or sending it by post, the beauty of the washi egg is enhanced if you cover a suitably sized, wooden or cardboard box with a piece of matching washi. You might like to make your own box following the instructions in this book. You can either line the box with plain washi or fit it out with colored straw.

A particularly lovely gesture for a very special occasion would be to cover and line the box with washi and then to nestle the washi egg in the folds of a pretty, lace handkerchief. This is thoughtfulness!

Washi Eggs as Christmas Ornaments

Suspended from a tiny gold or silver crown, washi eggs make delightful ornaments for the festive season, and will have your tree glowing with color. Of course, you aren't limited to hanging these ornaments only at Christmas, but can have them on display throughout the year, brightening up any corner of your home.

1. In a handicraft shop, ask for crowns or *okan* in Japanese. They are either silver – great for eggs with blue tones – or gold. They are 3/8" in diameter, are round, made of metal, look lacy and have a hole in the middle. Also buy some thin gold or silver cord.

2. Cut the cord to the desired length and thread both ends through the hole in the center of the crown, threading from the convex side, forming a loop. Tie a simple knot and pull the cord gently so that the knot disappears as far as it can into the crown. If too much cord is sticking out, simply cut it off.

3. Place a drop of strong glue around the knot and at the north pole of your egg. For me that is the pointed end. Some people like to hang them the other way round. Suit yourself. Applying the crown after the spooning stage will allow it to be embedded in the lacquer and thus be more durable.

4. Place the crown carefully at the center of the chosen end, press it down and hold it for a little while until you feel it will stay put. If you simply lay it down somewhere, there is a chance that the crown will slip with the weight of the cord and your priceless washi egg will be ruined.

If you can't find crowns, most handicraft shops sell small pearls which can be threaded in the same way. You can also tie a narrow ribbon around a toothpick that you have broken into a length about 3/4" (2cm) long. Push the toothpick and the knot through a hole in the egg and pull the ribbon upwards. The toothpick will wedge itself horizontally inside the egg.

Washi Eggs for Children

MATERIALS
Thin washi or colorful paper napkins
Egg blown in advance and thoroughly dry
Paste
Container for paste
Hair spray – optional
Bottle of lacquer
Small, medium-soft brush for lacquer
Spoon – optional

1. Sit your child down and show him or her how to tear off small pieces of washi approximately the size of your thumb nail. It is a good idea to keep the colors separate, making small piles of each.

2. Place a small container with some diluted paste on the table and invite the child to spread the paste thinly all over the top half of the egg. A plastic egg carton, cut into sections, makes economical containers for groups.

3. Supply each child with either a damp cloth or a paper towel. Have the child wipe his or her fingers clean and then place, one by one, the torn off pieces of washi over the pasted surface of the egg. The pieces can overlap a little. It isn't very critical.

4. Since the paper is tissue thin, it dries very quickly, so the process can be repeated at the other end almost immediately.

5. Being careful not to move the tiny pieces of washi, pat and roll the egg between your hands and use your thumb nail or the pads of your fingers to smooth the egg all over. You will probably find that the fine edges of the washi look fuzzy. To make them lie down, you can either place another very thin layer of paste all over the egg, or spray the egg with hair spray.

6. When the egg has dried somewhat, repeat the above using a contrasting colored washi. Don't try to completely cover the egg this time as it gives a very pretty effect to be able to see the first color peeping through. It doesn't matter how many layers you use.

7. When you are finished and the egg is as smooth as you can possibly manage, each child might like to add his or her name, written as small as possible, at one end of the egg. Although not crucial, the children could spoon their eggs at this stage. Then lacquer the egg just as you would the ones I have described above.

This is a fun idea for rainy days, for days when a child is recovering from an illness and unable to go out to play, or for a kindergarten teacher who could help her charges to make lovely presents to take home just in time for Easter.

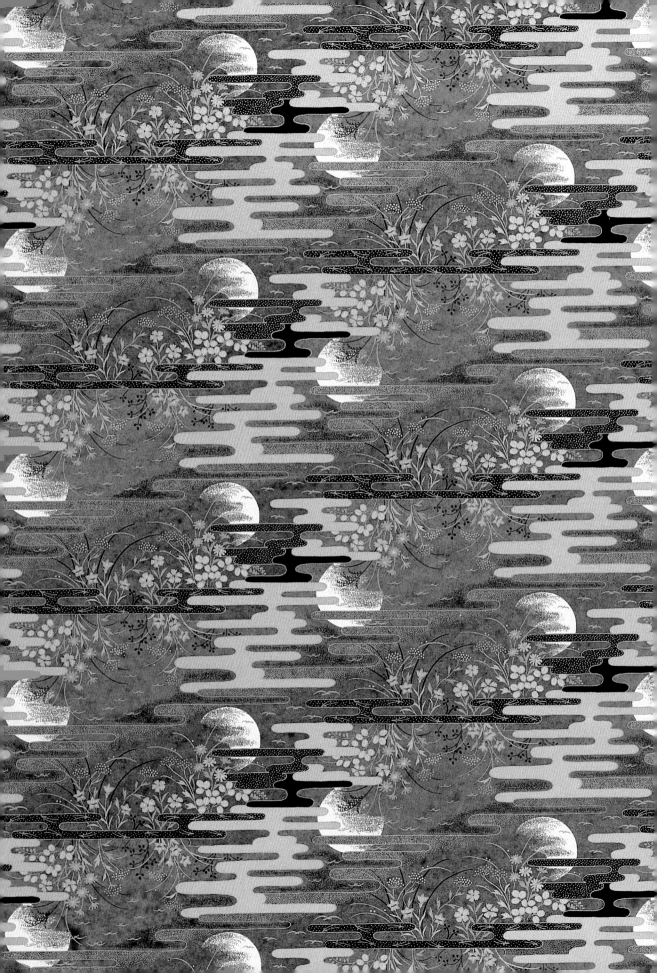

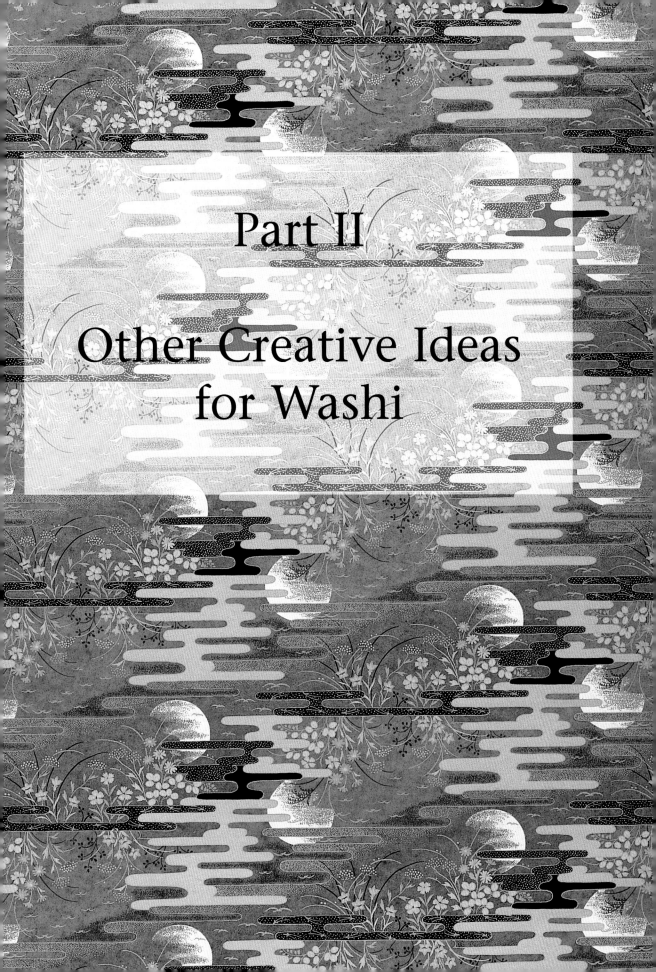

Part II

Other Creative Ideas
for Washi

Paperweight

MATERIALS
Stone, approximately 3¹/₂" x 2"
 (8cm x 5cm)
Small bottle of colored, glossy paint
Small paint brush
Small pieces of washi containing motif
Scissors
Household glue
Soup spoon
Lacquer
Small, medium-soft brush for lacquer

Using a stone as a base for showing off the beauty of washi is fun and easy. It can be used as a paper-weight or simply set out as an ornament.

I. Paint the Stone

Your stone need not be absolutely flat, but it should stand in a way that will show your motif clearly. To prepare the surface of the stone, I like to use black shiny paint, but any neutral color will do.

1. Scrub the stone well under running water and pat it dry.

2. Using a small paint brush and a small pot of gloss paint that can be found in an art supply or hobby shop, paint the upper surface of your stone. Before it dries, place it on a small elevated surface such as the top of a bottle and continue to paint the sides and a little of the underside part.

II. Apply the Washi and Finish

Go through your store of washi paper and choose a design that has a striking element such as a red camellia or a kabuki face. If you decide on a flower, cut out the surrounding green separately. If the top of the stone is not flat, two or three smaller pieces of washi are easier to work with than one large piece. Using smaller pieces, the washi will lie smoothly, without any crinkles.

1. Now cut out, very carefully, the motif you have chosen to use as decoration. Position the motif on the face of the stone and, using strong glue, glue on the decorative piece.

2. When it is dry, spoon the edges of the washi to achieve as smooth a surface as possible. Don't forget to work along the edges and press quite firmly.

3. Now lacquer the whole stone 2 or 3 times, remembering not to be too hasty.

Candle Shade

I am sure that once your friends see how lovely your next tea table looks when decorated with these delightful little candle shades, you will be kept busy making more for everyone.

MATERIALS

1/4 sheet of washi paper, approximately 12¹/2" x 19¹/4" (32cm x 49cm) /
Ruler / Straight-edged scissors / Fire-resistant liquid (sodium silicate) /
Ordinary household glue / Stiff cardboard for making template / Ordinary household knife /
Approximately 16" (40cm) ribbon, cord or wool / Needle with a large eye / Tea candles /
Small plate or coaster on which to place the tea candles

I. Make a Pattern

Before you begin, think about whether you would like to make several candle shades from the same patterned washi or whether perhaps you would prefer different patterns that are in the same tones. Making some out of patterned washi and one from plain washi is very pretty too. Once you have made one with me, you might like to experiment and make them all slightly different heights.

1. Trim the washi so that you have a large rectangle with clean edges. Before you continue, check to see if your washi pattern needs to run in one particular direction. A tree would look very odd if viewed upside down, for example. On the unpatterned side of your washi, make 3 or 4 pencil marks along one of the long edges, 1 1/4" (3cm) from the edge. Join the pencil marks by drawing a line across the washi.

2. From that line, measure another 2 3/4" (7cm) vertically and again make 3 or 4 pencil marks. Join those marks as you did a moment ago. The candle shade will be folded along the 1 1/4" (3cm) line. That fold will be at the top of your candle shade. I have made this fold so that when you sit at a tea table you will see the patterned washi inside as well as outside the shade.

3. Using either a paper cutter or a pair of straight sided scissors, cut along the second line.

You now have a rectangle 12 1/2" x 4" (32cm x 10cm).

4. Paint the rectangle with sodium silicate, a fire-resistant chemical which you will be able to buy in a drug store. There is no way to completely prevent paper from burning, but sodium silicate will prevent the paper from burning easily and would give you plenty of time to blow out the candle if an accident were to occur. Once it is dry, continue.

5. Fold the washi along the first pencil line so that the pattern is visible on both sides. The rectangle is now 12 1/2" x 2 3/4" (32cm x 7cm).

6. Glue the 1 1/4" (3cm) fold in place, using only a minimum of paste or glue to avoid excess stretching and leave it to dry.

You may like to measure a rectangle 12 1/2" x 5 1/2" (32cm x 14cm) instead of 12 1/2" x 4" (32cm x 10cm) as I have described. In this case you would fold your rectangle in half lengthwise. This version makes the candle shade as pretty on the inside as on the outside, but it might not shine as brightly as the first version.

II. Fan Fold

1. Cut a 4" x 1/2" (10cm x 1.2cm) strip of very stiff cardboard. Lay it across the narrow, 2 3/4" (7cm) end of the folded washi and be very careful that it is flush with the edge of the washi.

2. Using the back of a blunt knife, score a line on the washi, along the edge of the cardboard template. Repeat this step all the way along.

3. Fold along the scored lines, first one way and then the other, to the end. Press the accordion tightly.

4. On the patterned side, measure 3/8" (1cm) from the washi edge with no fold, and make a dot in the center of each fold of your accordion. If you want to thread some narrow ribbon through the holes later on, it is easier if you poke holes through these dots now. If you wish to trim your candle shade with a length of wool or thin cord that will fit through a large eyed needle, you can pierce the holes at the end.

5. You can now glue the accordion together along its 2 3/4" (7cm) edge to form a circle. Sometimes it will be necessary to cut off one of the folds in order to create a continuous accordion effect.

A pretty effect that would suit a candle shade made of plain washi is to cut tiny triangles out of the edges of the folds, either in a line around the middle or at different heights, when you reach step 4.

III. Decorate with Ribbon

1. Treat a ribbon or a piece of wool with sodium silicate and allow it to dry thoroughly.

2. Thread your ribbon through a pointed needle with a large eye. Beginning opposite the place where the accordion was glued together, pierce the washi through the dots or holes you made previously and weave in and out, backwards and forwards, until you are back at the beginning again. Pull the ribbon until the inner diameter of the candle shade is approximately the size of a tea candle. Ease the folds a little so that they are evenly placed.

3. Finally, drop your tea candle into the candle shade from the top and push it down until it rests on the table top. Adjust the ribbon so that the shade fits snugly and tie a bow. Cut off any excess ribbon.

IV. Finishing Touches

Since the tea candle is in a metal form, it will become quite hot and I recommend, therefore, that you place it on a small plate or coaster to protect the surface of your table.

Take the tea candle out of the shade to light it and place it in the shade carefully from the top. Voila!

Flower Vase

MATERIALS
Piece of thin cardboard,
  (about 1/16" [2mm] thick)
  approximately 6" x 3" (15cm x 8cm)
Ruler
Sharp pencil
43/4" (12cm) test tube or vial
Scissors to cut cardboard and
  a small pair of curved nail scissors
Semi-fine sandpaper (#600) – optional
Small piece of washi,
  at least 6" x 63/4" (15cm x 17cm)
Paste
Container for paste
Lacquer – optional
Small, medium-soft brush for
  lacquer – optional

*The simplicity of this little washi vase is amazing,
as is its beauty and practicality. I really look for-
ward to sharing this idea with you.*

I. Make a Cardboard Pattern

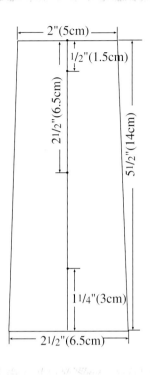

1. Draw a horizontal line 2″ (5cm) long at the top of your cardboard. Make a pencil mark in the middle of that line.

2. Draw a vertical line, 51/2″ (14cm) long, from the middle of the top line. At the end of that vertical line measure and draw a line 11/4″ (3cm) to the right and left of the vertical line (total length 21/2″ [6.5cm]).

3. Now join the ends of the top and bottom lines. So far so good!

4. From the top of the 51/2″ (14cm) long line measure and make a pencil mark 1/2″ (1.5cm) downward.

5. Again starting at the top of the 51/2″ (14cm) long line, measure 21/2″ (6.5cm) downward and make a pencil mark.

6. Starting at the bottom of the 51/2″ (14cm) long line this time, measure and make a pencil mark 11/4″ (3cm) upwards.

In reference to instruction 2, the vertical line (length of the vase) is always 3/4″ (2cm) longer than the test tube, so in this case 51/2″ (14cm). You can easily adjust this measurement to work with a test tube of another length.

II. Make a Figure Eight

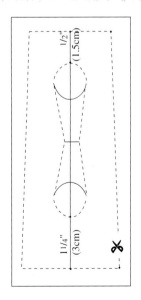

1. Place the opening of your test tube in the middle of the cardboard, immediately below the 1/2″ (1.5cm) pencil mark. Trace around it.

2. Do the same at the bottom but, this time, place the test tube above the 11/4″ (3cm) pencil mark.

3. Join the outer edges of the two circles, curving inward toward the 51/2″ (14cm) line. At the narrowest point the lines should be about 1/4″ (6mm) apart.

III. Cut Out the Frame

Cut around the outside edges of the frame. Then make a vertical slit between the two circles and cut toward one of the curved lines connecting the circles using a pair of sharp scissors that fit comfortably in your hand. When you reach a line, turn and continue to cut out the narrow space between the circles. Sandpaper all the cut edges. The vase, so far, is still flat!

IV. Make a Washi Pattern

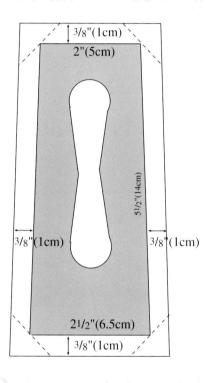

1. Look at your washi and decide if you want a particular part of the pattern to show on the vase. Then lay the cardboard frame on the plain side of your chosen washi, leaving at least 3/8″ (1cm) of space all around it, and trace the outer edges of the frame.

2. Measure 3/8″ (1cm) from several points around the outline you just drew, and join those points with a ruler. Then cut along the outer line.

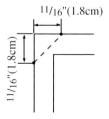

3. Corners should be 1/16″ (2mm) less than the sum total of their border. In our case, we have a border 3/8″ (1cm) wide on each side of the cardboard frame, which makes the sum total of the border 3/4″ (2cm). So when we want to mark the corners of the washi pattern, we should measure 11/16″ (1.8cm) horizontally and vertically from each corner and mark those points. Join each set of marks with a diagonal line. Cut along the lines across each corner. This will ensure tidy and non-bulky corners later on when you fold the washi.

V. Pasting

1. Using either your finger or a small brush that is 3/4" (2cm) wide, spread the paste onto the back of the washi pattern. Let it sink in for a moment and brush off any excess paste. Lay the cardboard vase on the washi pattern using the traced line as a guide. Turn it over and smooth out any air bubbles or excess paste.

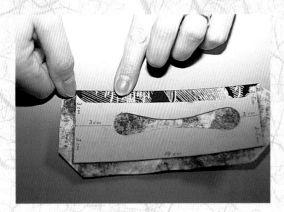

2. Turn back to the plain side of the washi and fold the long sides over first. Using the tip of your thumb, press down the part of the cut that is nearest to the corner. Next fold over the short sides.

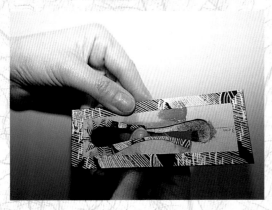

3. Make a vertical slit in the washi in the middle of the figure eight using a small pair of nail scissors. Cut towards and up to the cardboard in any direction and cut fringes of about 5mm wide all around. Fold over the fringes, one by one, to the other side and press them down. If the fringes have dried while you were working, simply add a little more paste.

4. Run your fingers or a blunt object such as your pencil over the inner edge of the figure eight to give it a smooth and clear cut look.

VI. Make the Back Piece

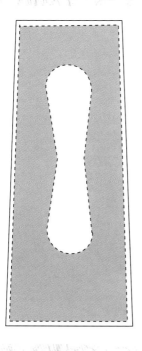

1. Place the cardboard on a second piece of washi and trace all around the outer edge and inside the figure eight. You will not need a border this time, so go ahead and cut out the second washi pattern including the figure eight. Since even the sharpest pencil has a certain thickness and since washi stretches a little when wet, cut slightly inside the pencil line when cutting the outer edge. Check the washi to be sure that it fits well and doesn't overlap. Slightly smaller is better than slightly too big.

2. Now spread paste all over the back of the washi, wait for a moment and then brush off any excess paste and place it carefully over the fringes.

3. You can either lay the damp vase between two towels or between several layers of newspaper. If you use newspaper, you should replace the newspapers two or three times. Place a heavy object on top such as a wooden cutting board piled high with heavy books and leave the vase to dry. This may take up to two days. And yes, the vase is still flat!

VII. Lacquering the Vase – Optional

Lacquering the washi surface will protect the vase from water damage and bring out the lovely colors that all washi have in common.

Use a clear drying lacquer and a small brush. Don't be in a hurry and be sure to keep the layers of lacquer as thin as possible. If you notice any tiny air bubbles on the surface of the lacquer, just brush them away with the same brush you are using. You can lacquer the first two layers within an hour of each other, but allow the lacquer to dry overnight before applying subsequent layers.

VIII. Finishing Touches

Place the bottom of the test tube first in the top hole from the front and then bend the frame gently and bring the test tube bottom back through the lower hole. Now add your favorite flower and you have the sweetest and most practical of flower vases that you can slip into a drawer when not in use!

When filling the test tube with water or changing the water, I suggest you take it out of the frame to protect the washi.

File

MATERIALS
2 pieces of cardboard, 1/16" (2mm) thick,
approximately 6" x 81/2" (15.5cm x 21.5cm)
Metal ruler
Pencil
Cutter & scissors
Cutting board – optional
Sandpaper or ordinary knife
1/4 sheet of washi, approximately 121/2" x
191/4" (32cm x 49cm)
1/4 sheet of washi in a contrasting color
Paste
Container for paste
Brush, 3/4" (2cm) wide – optional
Chisel, 3/8" (1cm) wide, and a
hammer – optional
5' (1.5m) of ribbon or cotton tape

This little file makes a very pretty present if you put some attractive writing paper and envelopes in it, or you might like to make it for yourself to keep special letters from days gone by.

I. Prepare the Cardboard

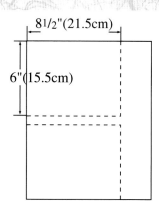

8¹/2"(21.5cm)

6"(15.5cm)

1. Measure carefully and draw 2 rectangles on the card-board, 8¹/2" x 6" (21.5cm x 15.5cm.)

2. Cut out the two pieces of cardboard with a cutter on a cutting board or thick layers of newspaper, and smooth the edges with either the back of a knife or with fine sandpaper if you happen to have some. I cut once, concentrating on cutting along the edge of my metal ruler. Then once more, still using the ruler as a guide, and pressing harder. If necessary, I'll cut again without the ruler.

II. Cut the Washi

For this file you can experiment with some of the bolder washi patterns. It will depend for whom you are making the file, but patterns with stunning kabuki faces or geometric designs look very original. For the inside covers, I like to use non-patterned washi. For example off-white washi with visible traces of fiber looks very noble.

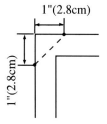

1"(2.8cm)

1"(2.8cm)

1. Lay the two cardboard rectangles on the plain side of the washi leaving at least 1" (2.8cm) between them. Trace around the edges of the cardboard.

2. You will need a border of 1/2" (1.5cm) all around each piece of cardboard. Measure 1/2" (1.5cm) at various points from the traced line and join those points using your pencil and a ruler. Then cut along the outer line using either a cutter or straight-edged scissors.

3. Measure 1" (2.8cm) horizontally and vertically from each corner and mark those points. Join each set of marks with a diagonal line. Cut along the lines across each corner. This will ensure tidy and non-bulky cor-ners when you fold the washi later on.

III. Pasting

1. Using either your finger or a small brush, 3/4" (2cm) wide, spread the paste onto the back side of one of the washi rectangles. Let it sink in for a moment and brush off any excess paste. Lay the cardboard on the plain side of the washi, using the traced line as a guide. Turn it over and smooth out any air bubbles or excess paste using the side of your hand or a wad of cloth.

2. Turn the cardboard over again, so that the plain side of the washi is facing you, and fold the long sides over first. Then, using the tip of your thumb, press down the part of the cut that is nearest to the corner. Fold over the short sides. Smooth the edges with a blunt object such as a knife or your thumb nail. Repeat the above for the second cover.

3. Lay the two pieces between two towels or between several layers of newspaper. The towels have the advantage that they are very absorbent. Whether you use newspapers or towels you should change them from time to time. Weigh them down. I use a big wooden chopping board and then I add as many heavy books as I can lay my hands on. Leave them that way for about two hours until they are partially dry.

Note: If you would like to add a decoration to your file, please see "Finishing Touches" at the end of this chapter before continuing. If you are happy with the beauty of the washi you have chosen, please continue.

IV. Cover Linings

1. While those two pieces of cardboard are drying, measure and cut two pieces of contrasting or plain washi that are 1/4" (5mm) smaller all around than the cardboard covers.

2. Spread some paste on one of the washi rectangles and lay it carefully on the inside of one of the cardboard covers.

3. Stroke the surface with the side of your hand or a wad of cloth to be sure it is smooth and repeat steps 2 and 3 with the other cover. Using a plastic bag as a glove works very well.

4. Now dry them again thoroughly between the towels or newspapers. This will take a day or two. Unless the covers are completely dry, they will curl up.

V. Make Slits for the Ribbon

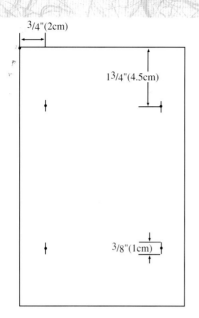

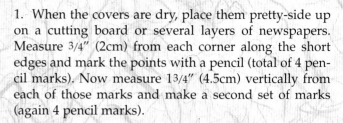

1. When the covers are dry, place them pretty-side up on a cutting board or several layers of newspapers. Measure 3/4" (2cm) from each corner along the short edges and mark the points with a pencil (total of 4 pencil marks). Now measure 13/4" (4.5cm) vertically from each of those marks and make a second set of marks (again 4 pencil marks).

2. Using your cutter and working from the patterned side, cut a 3/8" (1cm) long vertical slit at the 13/4" (4.5cm) marks. If you happen to have a sharp chisel that is 3/8" (1cm) wide, that is a good tool to make a clean slit. Put the cardboard cover on a wooden chopping board or a cutting board and place the chisel on the mark where the slit should be and give it a good whack with a hammer. Repeat this step on the left hand side of the front cover, and for the back cover.

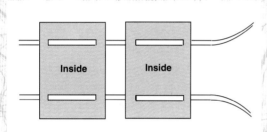

3. Cut the ribbon you are going to use in half and thread it through the slits as shown in the diagram.

VI. Finishing Touches

Covered Corner

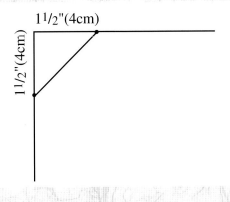

1. Cut a rectangle 4" x 1³/8" (10cm x 3.5cm) out of a plain piece of washi. A strong, plain colored thick washi usually looks best.

2. Fold the 4" x 1³/8" (10cm x 3.5cm) piece of plain washi in half and make a small mark on the edge on the crease.

3. Decide which corner you would like to decorate and measure 1¹/2" (4cm) horizontally and vertically from that corner and make two small marks. Join those two marks with a diagonal pencil line.

4. Spread some paste on the rectangle, wait a moment for the paste to sink in and brush off any excess. Working from the front or pretty side of the cover, lay one of the long edges of the washi strip along the pencil line you drew across the corner. Remember to place the center mark of the washi rectangle exactly over the corner. Turn the cover over and fold one side of the washi over. Then using the tip of your thumb, press down the part of the cut that is nearest to the corner. Fold over the other side. Press firmly.

In case you would like to make a larger or smaller corner for a different project, the following is a formula you can use to measure and cut a rectangle that will give you a neat corner: The size of the rectangle you need to cover a corner is always 1/16" (2mm) wider than the dotted line and 3/4" (2cm) longer than the double line.

Contrasting Edge

1. If you would like to add a contrasting edge to the front cover, measure and cut out a piece of thick, contrasting washi 1¹/4" x 8¹/2" (3cm x 22cm).

2. Fold the piece in half, lengthwise.

3. Spread some paste on its plain side and lay one half of it along one of the long edges. Lay it so that the crease is flush with the long edge and fold the other half over and press it to the inside of the cover and press firmly.

Photo File

MATERIALS

2 pieces of cardboard, 1^1/$_6$" (2mm) thick
  and at least 4^1/$_4$" x 6" (11cm x 15.5cm)
Metal Ruler
Pencil
Cutter and scissors
Cutting board–optional
Sandpaper or ordinary knife
^{1}/$_4$ sheet of washi, approximately
  12^1/$_2$" x 19^1/$_4$" (32cm x 49cm)
Paste
Container for paste
Brush, ^{3}/$_4$" (2cm) wide–optional
Chisel, ^{3}/$_8$" (1cm) wide, and a
  hammer–optional
16" (40cm) of ribbon or cotton tape
Brass or wooden curtain ring approximately
  ^{3}/$_4$" (2cm) in diameter
Stiff white or black paper 25" x 5^3/$_4$"
  (63cm x 14.5cm)
Glue

*This photo file is a pretty and practical variation on
the writing paper file I have just described. I am sure
a friend would be thrilled to receive a few photos
taken during a recent visit if presented this way.*

I. Prepare the Cardboard

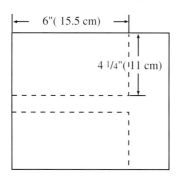

1. Measure carefully and draw 2 rectangles, 4¼" x 6" (11cm x 15.5cm), on ¹/16" (2mm) thick cardboard.

2. Cut out the two pieces of cardboard with a cutter on a cutting board or thick layers of newspaper and smooth the edges with either the back of a knife or fine sandpaper if you happen to have some. I cut once, concentrating on cutting along the edge of my metal ruler. Then once more, still using the ruler as a guide, and pressing harder. If necessary, I'll cut again without the ruler.

II. Cut the Washi

There is no one washi pattern that suits this project better than another. It will depend for whom you are making the file, but patterns with bold black and gold motifs look elegant whereas flowers in soft tones would surely please a girlfriend.

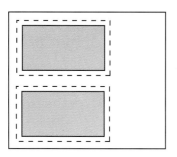

1. Lay the two cardboard rectangles on the plain side of the washi leaving at least 1¼" (3cm) between them. Trace around the edges of the cardboard. You will need a border of ¹/2" (1.5cm) all around each piece of cardboard. Measure ¹/2" (1.5cm) at various points around the traced line and join those points using your pencil and a ruler. Then cut along the outer line using either a cutter or straight-edged scissors, whichever you are most comfortable with.

2. Measure 1" (2.8cm) horizontally and vertically from each corner and mark those points. Join each set of marks with a diagonal line. Cut along the lines across each corner. This will ensure tidy and non-bulky corners later on when you fold the washi. (See sketch on page 47, Flower Vase Chapter, Step IV "Make a Washi Pattern," Instruction 3.)

III. Pasting

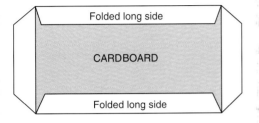

Folded long side

CARDBOARD

Folded long side

1. Using either your finger or a small brush, 3/4" (2cm) wide, spread the paste onto the plain side of one of the washi rectangles, let it sink in for a moment and brush off any excess paste. Lay the cardboard onto the plain side of the washi, using the traced line as a guide. Turn it over and smooth out any air bubbles or excess paste.

2. Turn back to the plain side of the washi and fold the long sides over first. Then, using the tip of your thumb, press down the part of the cut that is nearest to the corner.

3. Fold over the short sides. Smooth the edges with a blunt object such as a knife or your thumb nail.

4. Lay the two pieces between two towels or between several layers of newspaper. The towels have the advantage that they are very absorbent. Whichever you use, you should change them from time to time. Weigh them down. I use a big wooden chopping board and then I add as many heavy books as I can lay my hands on. Leave them to dry. This will be about 24 hours or longer.

IV. Make Slits for the Ribbon

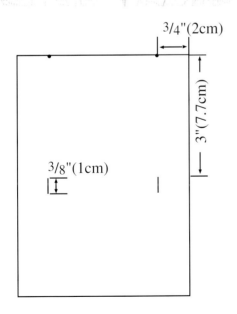

3/4"(2cm)

3"(7.7cm)

3/8"(1cm)

1. When the front cover is dry, measure 3/4" (2cm) along one of the short edges beginning from the right hand corner. Make a pencil mark. From that mark measure 3" (7.7cm) downward and make another mark. Using your cutter and working from the front or patterned side cut a vertical slit, 3/8" (1cm) long, at that mark. If you happen to have a sharp chisel that is 3/8" (1cm) wide, that is a good tool to make a clean-cut slit. Put the cardboard cover on a wooden chopping board or a cutting board and place the chisel on the mark where the slit should be and give it a good whack with a hammer.

2. Repeat this step on the left hand side of the front cover.

V. Thread the Ribbon

1. Thread one end of the ribbon from inside to outside through the right hand slit and pull it right through leaving approximately 1/2" (1.5cm) on the inside. Glue that short end to the inside of the cover with its end near the outer edge.

2. If you have a hammer, hit the short end of the ribbon once. This will flatten the ribbon and the slit beneath it.

3. On the outside, thread the long end of the ribbon through the brass or wooden ring and back through the same slit, from outside to inside.

4. Pull the ribbon so that the ring sits tightly on the outside of the cover. Using just a little glue, glue the long end of the ribbon across the inside of the cover and thread it through the opposite slit, from inside to outside.

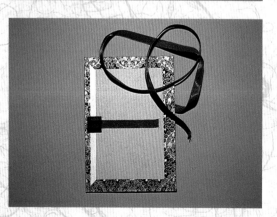

5. To really anchor the ribbon on the inside of the ring slit, cut a small square of strong washi no more than 1" (2.5cm) square and glue that over the ribbon end. Press firmly.

VI. Prepare the Accordion Fold

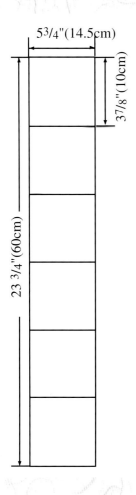

5 3/4"(14.5cm)

3 7/8"(10cm)

23 3/4"(60cm)

1. Using either black, white or any thick, plain-colored paper, measure and draw a rectangle 23 3/4" x 5 3/4" (60cm x 14.5cm). If your piece of cardboard is larger than the one we are working on right now, the accordion fold that will hold the photos should be 1/8" (5mm) smaller all round than the cover itself.

2. Along one of the long edges, measure and make tiny pencil marks every 3 7/8" (10cm). Repeat that step along the other long edge. Using your ruler as a guide, score a line between each set of marks. This makes it much easier to fold the paper. Fold the paper first one way and then the other at the places you have just marked.

3. I suggest you mix a few drops of strong glue into some paste, stir well, and spread the mixture over one of the end sections of the accordion fold.

4. Taking care to place it centrally, glue that section to the inside of the front cover. Wipe off any excess paste that might ooze out of the edges.

5. Spread the glue/paste mixture over the other end section and paste it over the inside of the back cover. Again make sure that you clean away any excess paste. Leave the accordion open and weigh each cover down with something heavy and leave them to dry completely.

VII. Finishing Touches

1. If you now glue in the photos you have chosen and fold the ribbon around the back of the photo file to the front, you will, I am sure, be both proud and happy with your new photo file.

2. Thread the ribbon from underneath up through the ring, then up and over the ribbon and down through the circle you have created. More simply said, tie the ribbon loosely. The ribbon is just there to prevent the accordion from opening and spilling its contents.

Mirror Frame

MATERIALS
2 pieces of cardboard, 1/16" (2mm) thick,
  at least 6" x 81/4" (15cm x 21cm) each
Ruler
Pencil
Cutter and scissors
A cutting board – optional
Sandpaper – optional
Mirror, 1/16" (2mm) thick, 4" x 4"
  (10cm x 10cm)
1/4 sheet of washi, approximately
  121/2" x 191/4" (32cm x 49cm)
Paste
Container for paste
Glue
Lacquer – optional
Small brush for lacquer – optional

A good friend of mine gave me a little mirror frame covered in paper that she had made herself. It was delightful. I placed a tiny arrangement of handmade flowers in front of it, just off to one side, and the combination of the washi and the mirror reflecting the flowers is really beautiful.

I. Prepare the Cardboard

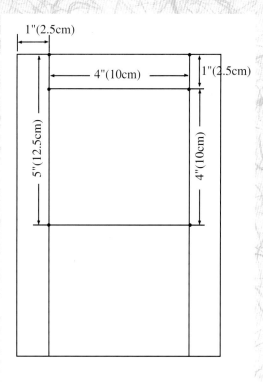

1"(2.5cm)

4"(10cm)

1"(2.5cm)

5"(12.5cm)

4"(10cm)

1. For this project you need to be as accurate as possible. Begin by cutting a rectangle from the cardboard that is 6" x 8¼" (15cm x 21cm). Smooth the edges with sandpaper, if you happen to have some, or with the edge of a blunt knife. This will be the back of the frame.

2. The front of the frame starts off the same way as the back. Measure and cut out a rectangle from the cardboard that is 6" x 8¼" (15cm x 21cm).

3. In order to prepare the hole into which you will place the mirror later on, measure 1" (2.5cm) horizontally from the left top corner of the rectangle and again 1" (2.5cm) horizontally from the right top corner and make a pencil mark. Do the same at the bottom edge.

4. Join the top and bottom marks by drawing a line between the two points.

5. Now measure 1" (2.5cm) down from the top edge and make a mark on the pencil line you drew a moment ago. Do this on both lines. Join the two points by drawing a horizontal pencil line.

6. Repeat this step, but this time measure 5" (12.5cm) down from the top edge and make a mark on the two vertical pencil lines. Join the two points with a horizontal pencil line. You have now drawn a square 4" x 4" (10cm x 10cm) into which you will place the mirror later on.

7. Using your ruler as a guide, cut out the square with a cutter.

8. Check the fit of the mirror you have had cut for you and adjust the size of the cardboard hole if necessary by paring off thin slivers of cardboard. If the difference is only minimal, you could probably make the mirror fit by sandpapering the inner edges of the square.

II. Prepare the Washi

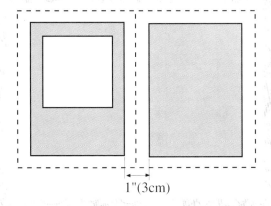

1"(3cm)

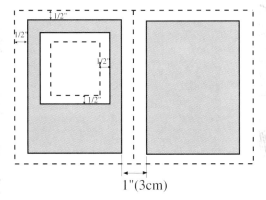

1"(3cm)

1. Lay both cardboard rectangles on the non-patterned side of the washi, leaving at least 1" (3cm) between them. Trace around the cardboard. You will need a border of 1/2" (1.5cm) all around each piece of cardboard. Measure 1/2" (1.5cm) at various points around the traced line and join those points using your pencil and a ruler. Then cut along the outer line.

2. One rectangle will cover the piece of cardboard without a hole which is the back of the frame. Lay it aside.

3. Now trace around the inside edges of the 4" x 4" (10cm x 10cm) square and lift off the cardboard.

4. Working inside the square, measure 1/2" (1.5cm) from all sides at various points and join those points with pencil lines. You now have a square within a square.

5. Using a cutter or a pair of scissors, cut an X in the middle of the inner square and cut towards a line. When you reach that line, turn your cutter or scissors and continue to cut along the line until you have cut out the inner square.

6. At each corner cut a slit towards the corner of the first square you drew.

7. Measure 1" (2.8cm) horizontally and vertically from each outer corner and mark those points. Join each set of marks with a diagonal line. Cut along the lines across each corner. This will ensure tidy and non-bulky corners later on when you fold the washi. (See sketch on page 47, Flower Vase Chapter, Step IV "Make a Washi Pattern," Instruction 3.)

III. Pasting

Spread the paste onto the back of the first washi rectangle you made. Lay the cardboard without a hole onto the plain side of the washi, using the traced line as a guide. Turn it over and smooth out any air bubbles or excess paste. Using a plastic bag as a glove works well. Turn back to the plain side of the washi and fold the long sides over first. Then using the tip of your thumb, press down the part of the cut that is nearest to the corner. Fold over the short sides. Repeat the above for the piece of cardboard that has a hole in it. Fold over the edges of the inner square as well.

IV. Final Assembly

Using a strong household glue, glue the two pieces of washi-covered cardboard together, uncovered sides facing. Be sure to align the edges quickly as glue does not give you as much time to slip and slide as does paste. And now for the magical moment. Clean your mirror piece and glue it in to the hole prepared for it.

V. Lacquering–Optional

You can create a pretty finish by brushing several layers of clear drying lacquer on to the front of the mirror frame. I suggest you use 3 or 4 layers of lacquer, keep the layers as thin as possible and be sure to leave ample time between layers for the lacquer to dry well. Isn't your mirror frame pretty? I also like the idea of lacquering just a section of the frame. For example, try lacquering only the section below the mirror. To achieve a smooth line on either side of the mirror, use a piece of cardboard as a guide.

VI. Make a Stand – Optional

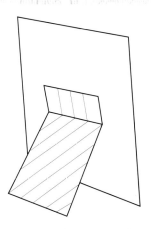

1. Cut out a piece of 1/16″ (2mm) thick cardboard that is 6″ x 4″ (15cm x 10cm). Measure 1″ (2.5cm) down from one end and draw a horizontal line across the cardboard.

2. Using a cutter and a ruler, score along that line, being careful not to press too hard. You do not want to cut through the cardboard, only crease it. Now bend the cardboard along the crease.

3. Using the knowledge you have gained by making the mirror frame, cut out a piece of washi that is 1/2″ (1.5cm) larger than the piece of cardboard all around.

4. Prepare the corners as described above, spread some paste on the plain side of the washi and lay the cardboard on the washi. Smooth out any air bubbles and fold over the long edges first and then the short sides.

5. Cut out another piece of washi that is the exact size of the cardboard stand, 6″ x 4″ (15cm x 10cm). Paste it and lay it carefully on the uncovered side of the stand. Once again, bend the stand gently at the crease you made earlier on.

6. Straighten out the stand and dry it between two towels or between newspapers. When it is completely dry use a strong household glue to glue the stand in place on the back of your mirror frame, being careful to check the height first so that the frame stands at an angle that is pleasing to you. Only glue the 1″ x 4″ (2.5cm x 10cm) area.

If you intend to hang your mirror frame, you can buy single hanging parts that will glue onto the back of your frame

Lamp Shade

MATERIALS
Plain, smooth lamp shade
 – old or new
Plain paper
Pencil
Ruler
Scotch tape
Scissors
Washi – 1/4 sheet for this project,
 approximately 12 1/2" x 19 1/4"
 (32cm x 49cm)
Paste
Container for paste
Glue
Cord or cloth bias tape – optional

*I am sure the lovely effect of light shining through
your favorite washi will bring you pleasure every
time you switch on the lamp.*

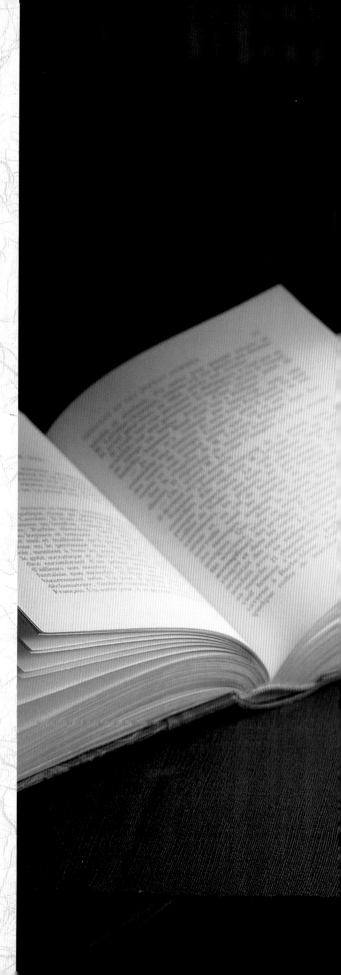

The lamp shade you are using must be a plain one. If you have an old lamp shade that is patterned or damaged but which otherwise suits your needs, you can take off the old cover and work with just the lamp shade frame. I will give instructions on how to do that at the end of this chapter. The lamp shade I am using to demonstrate this technique has a circumference of 8" (20cm) at the bottom, 2 3/4" (7cm) at the top and is 4 3/4" (12.3cm) high.

I. Trace a Pattern

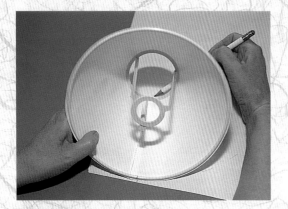

1. First of all make a mark on the inner, lower edge of the lamp shade, preferably on the seam.

2. Using any plain paper you have at home or even a newspaper, make a pattern as follows: lay your lamp shade on its side, near the lower left edge of the paper. Make a mark on the paper opposite the mark you made on the lamp shade a moment ago.

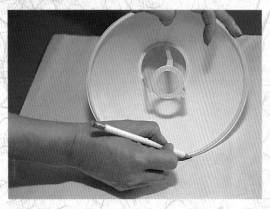

3. Now begin to roll the lamp shade across the paper while tracing along the bottom edge of the shade with your pencil. Keep rolling and tracing until you arrive at the beginning, i.e. your pencil mark.

4. Using your ruler and a pencil, make several marks 4 3/4" (12.3cm) from and at right angles to the traced line. Remember that the lampshade I am covering is 4 3/4" (12.3cm) high. Yours will probably be different. Join those pencil marks free hand

5. Now draw a straight pencil line at both ends to join the upper and lower edges of the lamp shade pattern.

Note: In our case, the pattern will look like a curved rectangle, but if the shade you are covering is almost the same size at the top and bottom, the pattern will look like a long rectangle.

II. Cut Out the Pattern

1. To make it easier for yourself to trim the pattern at the top, attach the pattern to the lamp shade along the bottom edge with small pieces of Scotch tape. Make sure that the bottom of the pattern is flush with the bottom of the lamp shade. Do this all around.

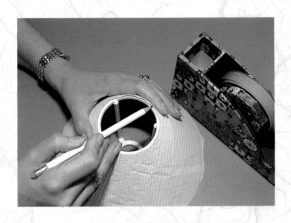

2. Your pattern may or may not be the right size at this stage. To be sure, place the lamp shade on the table, right way up and, using a pencil, make marks on the inside of the paper, flush with the top of the frame.

3. Before you take the pattern off the shade to trim it, take a look at the seam. The edge you started to roll from will be straight. Measure and make a couple of faint pencil marks 3/8" (1cm) inward along that short edge, i.e. the seam.

4. Then lay the second edge over it, fold it back and press the fold in line with the pencil marks.

5. Remove the pattern from the lamp shade and cut off the excess paper along the fold.

6. Cut off any excess paper around the top edge. The most difficult part of making this pretty lamp shade is now finished.

III. Prepare the Washi

For this project, a pattern that is repetitive, such as small flowers, works best. Stripes and patterns with a scene should be avoided. I also recommend that you hold the paper you would like to use up to a light, as some papers and patterns look better than others when the light shines through them.

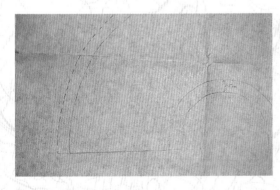

1. First of all, lay your paper pattern on the front side of the washi and, lifting up the ends and edges of the pattern, check once again that the design will not look warped when cut.

2. Turn the washi over so that the back side faces upwards. Lay the paper pattern on it and trace all around it with your pencil. Leave a border of at least 1/2" (1.5cm) all around the pattern.

3. Remove the pattern and, again using your pencil and a ruler, add a 1/2" (1.5cm) border at the top and bottom of the pattern. To do this, measure 1/2" (1.5cm) at several points from the top and bottom edges. Join those points free hand.

4. Cut out the washi shape along the outer edges.

IV. Paste the Washi

1. Using your finger, or a brush that is 3/4" (2cm) wide, cover the back side of the washi in paste and brush off any excess paste.

2. Being careful to lay the washi seam over the seam on your original lamp shade, quickly wrap the washi around the lamp shade. Don't hesitate to lift and re-lay the washi as often as needed. Smooth out any air pockets and push the washi this way and that until it is fairly smooth. The washi will have stretched quite a lot but this is normal. When you are satisfied that the washi will dry smoothly and that all major wrinkles have been smoothed away, leave the lampshade to dry for a while.

3. Now measure and make marks on the back side of the washi 1/2" (1.5cm) from the frame at the top and the bottom and trim off any excess paper.

4. Cut fringes about 3/8" (1cm) apart and at right angles to the edge of the frame. If you are covering a large lamp shade, you can cut the fringes about 3/4" (2cm) apart.

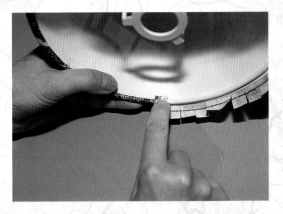

5. Working with only about 4 or 5 fringes at a time, spread a little household glue on the fringes and wrap them around the lampshade frame using your forefinger.

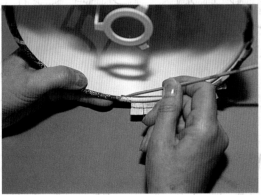

6. To give the edge a clean finish, use a toothpick, cake tester or another pointed object to press the fringes around and down behind the rim.

Working with the Frame Only

1. Buy paper that is specifically made for covering lamp shades. You may find it at either a handicraft shop or a lamp shade maker. It is fairly stiff and is adhesive on one side.

2. Make a paper pattern as described on page 70, lay the pattern on the adhesive paper and cut it out. You will not need a border. Peel off the protective foil and place the adhesive paper, sticky side down, onto the back side of your chosen washi. Work carefully so that there are no wrinkles. Cut the washi flush with the edge of the adhesive paper pattern.

3. Glue all around the outer edges of both the top and the bottom of the frame and place your stiff pattern around the frame. If you have measured correctly, the pattern should fit perfectly but it often doesn't. Don't worry. As long as the washi covers the frame all over, wait for the glue to dry and simply trim the excess washi with a pair of sharp scissors.

Album

MATERIALS
2 pieces of cardboard, 1/16" (2mm) thick,
  8" x 12" (20cm x 30cm),
  and 1 piece 3/4" x 8" (2cm x 20cm)
  or 1 large piece from which you can cut
  the above 3 pieces
Cutting board
Metal ruler
Pencil
Cutter & scissors
Medium-fine sandpaper
Hole puncher
Pointed scissors
1/2 sheet of washi, approximately
  121/2" x 38" (31.5cm x 97cm)
Paste
Container for paste
Glue
Brush, 3/4" (2cm) wide – optional
1/3 sheet of plain washi,
  121/2" x 243/4" (31.5cm x 63cm)
3 sheets of DIN A3 thick white paper or
  12 stiff photo album sheets,
  73/4" x 121/2" (19.5cm x 31.5cm)
2 book screws 1.5cm long

This project is special. It is a little more adventurous than the others I have written about but the end result is both professional and unique. I know you will enjoy it.

74

I. Prepare the Cardboard

Some art supply stores or stores that specialize in book maker products will cut the cardboard you need to your specifications. If cutting cardboard by hand, always use a new blade on your cutter in order to get the clean, sharp edges necessary for this project.

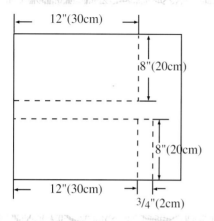

1. Accurately measure 2 rectangles, 8" x 12 " (20cm x 30cm) each, and one strip of cardboard 3/4" x 8" (2cm x 20cm).

2. Lay the cardboard on a cutting board or on a thick layer of newspapers and, using a medium length ruler as a guide, cut along the edges of each cardboard piece with a cutter. Press firmly. If you don't cut right through the cardboard the first time you can go back and cut through the second or third time, still using the ruler as a guide. If the edges are not smooth, you can either rub them with sandpaper or shave off fine slivers of cardboard with your cutter.

II. Construct a Template and Make Holes in the Covers

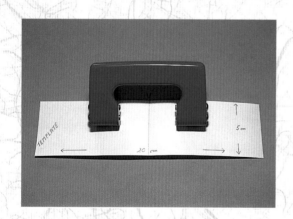

1. Measure and cut out a rectangle 2" x 8" (5cm x 20cm) from any piece of paper. Fold it in half and pinch the fold to mark the middle. Place the template in a hole puncher – two hole type – and place the pinched fold opposite the arrow or marker on the hole puncher. Punch two holes.

2. Measure 4" (10cm) along the short edge of one of the two large pieces of cardboard and make a mark.

3. Place the fold of the template on top of the mark you just made and trace around the inside of the two holes in the template.

4. Using the tips of pointed scissors or a special cardboard hole puncher, bore two holes in the cardboard. It doesn't matter too much if the holes aren't perfectly round. You can smooth any bumpy edges by pressing down on them with a blunt object and they will be covered by washi later on. The holes should be just big enough for the two book screws to fit through snugly.

III. Prepare the Washi

Since this object is bigger than the other things I have written about up to now, you might like to use a washi pattern that has a large design on it. You must also decide which part of the design you want to place where on the cover. Also be sure to check whether your washi has a pattern that should be viewed from one direction. In this case mark the back side of the washi with an arrow showing the direction of your pattern.

1. Cut off the white edges of the washi, being careful to create 90 degree corners and therefore parallel edges. (An L-shaped ruler is very useful for this purpose but it is not essential.)

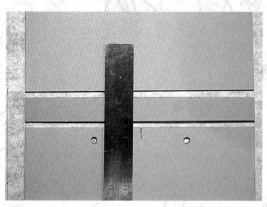

2. Lay the 3 cardboard pieces on the back side of your 1/2 sheet of chosen washi. Leave 3/16" (5mm) between the covers and the narrow strip that will form the spine of your album. Trace around the outside of the cardboard pieces.

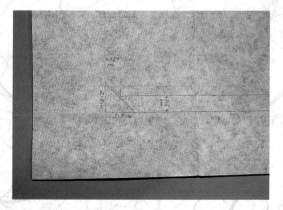

3. Measure and make a number of marks 1/2" (1.5cm) out from the line you have just traced. Join these together, using your pencil and a ruler, to form a continuous border. Then cut along this outer line only – not between the covers and the spine.

4. Measure 1" (2.8cm) horizontally and vertically from each corner and mark those points. Join each set of marks with a diagonal line. Cut along the lines across each corner. This will ensure tidy and non-bulky corners later on when you fold the washi. (See sketch on page 47, Flower Vase Chapter, Step IV "Make a Washi Pattern," Instruction 3.)

IV. Pasting

1. Prepare your paste according to the instructions. I like to add a few drops of strong glue to the paste for added strength

2. Using a brush that is 3/4" (2cm) wide, spread the paste onto the plain or back side of the large washi rectangle. It is a good idea to spread the paste from the middle towards the outer edges. Let it sink in for a moment and brush off any excess paste.

3. Lay the three cardboard pieces onto the plain side of the washi, using the traced lines as a guide. Press and rub all over the cardboard pieces to smooth the washi beneath. Fold the long sides over first and then using the tip of your thumb, press down the part of the cut that is nearest to the corner. Fold over the short sides.

4. Pick up the washi-covered cardboard pieces and turn them over carefully, pretty-side up. Using a blunt object, press gently between the covers and the album spine. Don't drag the blunt object or the wet washi may tear.

V. Prepare the Washi for the Spine

1. Using the same patterned washi as before, measure and cut out a strip 2 1/2" x 8 3/4" (6cm x 22cm).

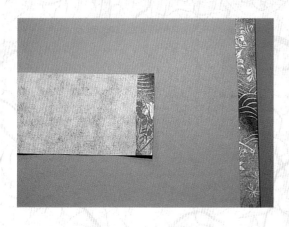

2. Measure 1/2" (1.3cm) from both short ends and fold them over. Using only very little paste, glue the fold down.

3. Spread the paste over the back side of the washi strip and place it, patterned side up, on the spine, leaving approximately 1/8" (3mm) at both ends free.

4. With a blunt object, press the washi down on both sides of the spine. Again, remember not to drag your blunt object.

Note: If you would like to decorate the front cover, for example with a contrasting-colored corner, see "Finishing Touches" at the end of this chapter before continuing.

VI. Prepare the Cover Linings

1. Working with the plain washi, measure and cut out two rectangles 7 1/2" x 11 1/2" (19.4cm x 29.4cm).

2. Apply the paste on the back side of one of the rectangles, give it time to soak in and brush off any excess paste. Then very carefully center it and lay it on the inside of the cover, leaving approximately 1.8" (3mm) free all around. If you don't get it right the first time, don't panic. Simply lift it off and try again. Washi is amazingly resilient.

3. Smooth out any excess paste using the side of your hand – using a plastic bag as a glove works well – and remove it with a damp cloth if it oozes out at the edges.

4. Repeat the above for the inside of the other cover.

5. Now feel where the holes are in the first cover you covered, and poke from the outside to inside through the washi with a sharp object.

6. Place both covers either between two towels or between several layers of newspaper, weigh them down with a heavy board and load some books on top of that. Leave them to dry. Whether you have used newspaper or towels, be sure to change them 2 or 3 times. The drying process will take at least 24 hours. Longer is better.

VII. Prepare the Album Sheets

If you would like to add more sheets, buy longer screws. If you decide to do this, however, remember to widen the strip of cardboard and the washi you cut for the spine. If you do not feel confident using a cutter, use a sharp pair of straight edged scissors. For your photo album to look as professional as possible, it is important that the edges be clean cut.

1. Whether you have bought thick, heavy duty album sheets or 3 large sheets of thick paper, measure 12 sheets of 7 3/4" x 12 1/2" (19.5cm x 31.5cm).

2. Using your ruler as a guide and a cutter, cut out each page.

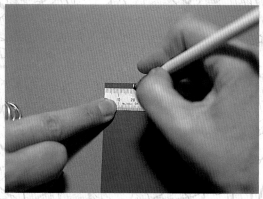

3. Place the first page horizontally in front of you. From the top left corner, measure 3/4" (2cm) horizontally along the top edge and make a mark.

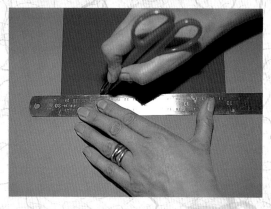

4. Do the same from the bottom left corner. Join the two marks with a faint pencil line. Using the tips of your scissors, score along that faint pencil line. Fold the paper along the scored line and paste it down using about 5 small dots of paste spread along the fold.

5. Keep some pressure on the glued fold for about a minute using all your fingers. When it is dry, bend the fold with your thumbs on one side and the remaining fingers on the other. Repeat steps 3-5 for remaining pages.

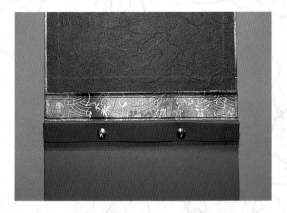

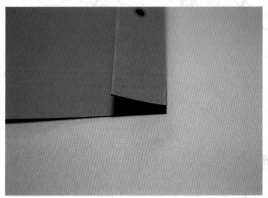

6. You could leave it at that but whereas the first pages would open easily, the last few pages would bulge and be difficult to hold open. I suggest, therefore, that you again measure horizontally from the top left corner, first 1″ (2.5cm) and from the same starting point, 1 1/4″ (3cm) and make pencil marks. Do the same from the bottom left corner. This time do not join the marks with a pencil line but using your ruler as a guide, score a line between each set of marks. Fold the page along those scored lines in the same direction.

VIII. Prepare Holes in the Album Sheets

1. Measure and make a very faint pencil mark in the middle of each short folded edge.

2. Place that mark against the arrow on the hole puncher and punch 2 holes.

3. Repeat this step for all remaining pages.

IX. Final Assembly

1. When the covers are dry, put in the long part of the book screw from the outside to the inside, place the sheets, folded side up, on the screws and screw on the top part of the screw.

2. All you need to do now is to decide which photos to include and to paste them into your album. Each sheet will hold either two 3 1/2″ x 5 1/8″ (9cm x 13cm) photos or four 2 1/4″ x 3 1/2″ (6cm x 9cm) sized photos per page. I wish I could see your finished album. I am sure it is very pretty indeed. Enjoy!

X. Finishing Touches

Covered Corner

1. Cut a rectangle 2" x 4 3/4" (5.2cm x 12cm) out of a plain piece of washi. A strong color and thick washi usually look best.

2. Decide which corner you would like to decorate and measure 2 3/4 (7cm) horizontally and vertically from that corner and make two small marks. Join those two marks with a faint pencil line. (Refer to sketch on page 55, File Chapter, Step VI "Covered Corner.")

3. Fold the 2" x 4 3/4" (5.2cm x 12cm) piece of plain washi in half and make a small mark on the crease.

4. Spread some paste on the rectangle, wait a moment for the paste to sink in and brush off any excess paste. Working from the front or pretty side of the cover, lay one of the long edges of the washi strip along the pencil line you drew across the corner. Remember to place the center mark of the washi strip exactly over the corner. Turn the cover over and fold one side of the washi over. Then using the tip of your thumb, press down the part of the cut that is nearest to the corner. Fold over the other side. Press firmly.

Contrasting Edge

1. Cut out a piece of contrasting, thick washi 1 1/2" x 8" (4cm x 20cm).

2. Fold that piece in half lengthwise.

3. Spread some paste on its plain side and lay one half of it along one of the short edges. Lay it so that the crease is flush with the short edge and fold the other half over and press it firmly to the inside of the cover.

Recycled Album

Materials
Two coins and/or a screwdriver
Full sheet of washi, 25½" x 38" (65cm x 97cm)
½ sheet of same or contrasting washi, 12½" x 38" (32cm x 97cm)
Pencil / Ruler / Cutter or scissors
Paste / Container for paste / Strong glue – optional
Brush, 3/4" (2cm) wide

This is a variation on the album I have described above, and a great way to economize. Try the following and I am sure you will soon be surprising your family and friends with unique and very beautiful albums as gifts.

1. Look for the type of album which has covers that can be unscrewed to allow additional pages to be inserted. The screws are on the inside of the front and back covers.

2. Start by unscrewing the two covers. It may be necessary to hold the back screw steady using a coin while you unscrew the front screw with either a coin or a small screwdriver. Remove the two covers and the back rib. Lay each cover in turn on the plain side of the washi sheet of your choice. Trace a pencil line around each cover leaving a border of 3/4" (2cm) all around. Cut out the washi pattern. Now lay the rib of the album on a leftover piece of washi and leave a margin of 3/4" (2cm) at each end. Cut it out.

3. Prepare your paste as directed, adding a few drops of glue to make it stronger.

4. Using a brush 3/4" (2cm) wide, apply the paste liberally to the non-patterned or back side of one piece of washi. It is best to work from the middle towards the outside. Allow time for it to soak in, and then either add a little more paste if it shows signs of being dry in patches or remove any excess paste that looks as though it might dry in ridges.

5. Lay the cover you are working with, right side down, in the middle of the washi and then pick up both the cover and washi. Turn them over and smooth the surface with your fingers or the heel of your hand.

6. Measure 1 1/2" (3.8cm) horizontally and vertically from each corner and mark those points. Join each set of marks with a diagonal line. Cut along the lines across each corner. This will ensure tidy and non-bulky corners later on when you fold the washi. (See sketch on page 47, Flower Vase Chapter, Step IV "Make a Washi Pattern," Instruction 3.)

7. Fold the long edges over first and then the shorter edge. At the corners, form as clean a fold as possible. On the inner side of the rib, fold the edge over and tuck it in to the slit that is formed by the cover and the rigid piece through which the screws must fit. This will be obvious once you are actually making the album. Repeat the above for the second cover.

8. Apply paste to the piece of washi that will cover the rib of the album and lay the rib on the washi, right side down and fold the overlapping pieces at both ends. Depending on the album design, it may be necessary to adjust the design by cutting off a piece of washi on all four corners. Remember to smooth the surface of each piece quickly and thoroughly.

9. When both covers have dried, measure the inside surface minus about 1/4" (5mm). Transfer this measurement to the back of either a matching piece of washi or a non-patterned white sheet. To avoid seeing the pencil line on the pretty side, cut just inside the pencil line.

10. Again, apply paste to this square on the back side, give it time to soak in, then very carefully center it and lay it on the inside of the cover. I hold one edge with two hands and lay it down first. Allowing my hands to glide down the sides of the paper, I lay the remaining part of the sheet. Smooth out any excess paste using the side of your hand and remove it with a damp cloth if it oozes out at the edges.

11. When all surfaces have dried, simply reassemble the album in the same way you took it apart. You will be amazed and thrilled at how your ugly duckling from the sale the week before has been transformed into a luxury album anyone would be proud to own.

Variation of Album

Although in the next chapter I describe how to make a box from scratch, a charming idea for making a very pretty gift box for a good friend is to attach the bottom of a white box to the spine and covers of the Album. There is no need for book screws and holes. Here are a few tips to help you along:

1. The covers are 3/8" (1cm) longer than the long edges of the box, and 3/16" (5mm) longer than the short edges.

2. The spine must be as wide as the box is high.

3. Make small slits in the center of the long edges of the covers. Thread a ribbon from outside to inside on each cover and glue them flat before adding cover linings. Tying the ribbons will enable you to close the lid of the box.

4. Glue the white box to the inside of one of the covers.

Box

MATERIALS

1 piece of cardboard, 1/16" (2mm) thick,
  25" x 25" (60cm x 60cm)
Metal ruler, 20" (50cm) or longer
Pencil
Cutter and cutting board
Scotch tape
Strong glue
Fine sandpaper
1 piece of thin cardboard, approximately
  6½" x 8½" (16cm x 21cm)
¼ sheet of plain washi,
  12½" x 19¼" (32cm x 49cm)
Paste
Container for paste
Brush, 3/4" (2cm) wide
¼ sheet of patterned washi
  12½" x 19¼" (32cm x 49cm)
10 metal clamps,
  approximately 3/4" (2cm) wide

This sounds so simple, but in fact, this is quite a challenging project. Once you have mastered the basics of making a box, you will find many occasions when a box, made to measure, makes all the difference to a present or a particular need.

I. Prepare the Cardboard

It is very important that you cut out the cardboard parts cleanly and precisely. If the shop where you buy your cardboard is equipped to cut cardboard to size, please take advantage of their professional cutter. If not, be as exact as possible. I recommend that you break off the last section of your cutter, to be sure that you have the sharpest cutting blade possible. Don't be in a hurry. If you make a mistake, don't try and make do. Treat yourself to a second or third try. I assure you that the box we are going to make together will be worth the extra cardboard.

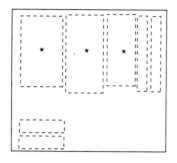

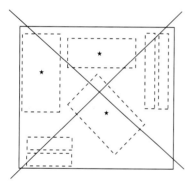

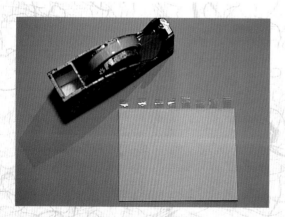

1. Measure and draw the following rectangles on the 25″ x 25″ (60cm x 60cm) piece of cardboard:

* 1 piece 6″ x 8″ (15cm x 20cm) – bottom of box

* 1 piece 6 1/8″ x 8 1/8″ (15.4cm x 20.4cm) – lid

* 1 piece 5 7/8″ x 7 7/8″ (14.6cm x 19.6cm) – inner lid

2 pieces 1 1/4″ x 8″ (3cm x 20cm) – long sides of box

2 pieces 1 1/4″ x 6 1/8″ (3cm x 15.4cm) – short sides of box

2. It is most important that the pieces marked with a star be laid out side by side. Cardboard and non-hand-made paper bends in one direction more easily than the other. Two pieces that bend in different directions will never dry flat when glued together.

3. Using your ruler as a guide, press firmly both on the ruler and the cutter and cut out the 7 cardboard pieces. I cut once, concentrating on cutting along the edge of my metal ruler. Then once more, still using the ruler as a guide, and pressing harder.

4. Pick up the piece that is 6″ x 8″ (15cm x 20cm). It will be the bottom of your box. Attach short pieces of Scotch tape, about 1 1/2″ (4cm) long and about 3/4″ (2cm) apart, all around the cardboard. (These strips of Scotch tape will keep the sides of the box secure until the glue dries later on.)

II. Glue the Pieces Together

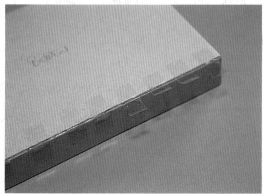

1. Before you continue, check to be sure that the four narrow pieces of cardboard are exactly the length of the sides of the box. Remember that the two short pieces will be 1/8″ (4mm) longer than the short edge of the bottom of the box. If they are even a little bit different in length, pare off the difference with the cutter.

2. Now spread strong glue along the outside edges of the long sides of the bottom. I put a little glue on a saucer and dip a toothpick into the glue to apply it carefully to the edges.

3. Pick up one of the long, narrow pieces of cardboard – 1 1/4″ x 8″ (3cm x 20cm) – and lay it up against the glued, outside edge of the bottom. Not on it. Press it against the bottom and hold it for a moment. Now lift up the strips of Scotch tape and press them against the side of the box.

Repeat the above for the second long, narrow piece of cardboard.

4. Spread the strong glue along the outside edges of the short sides of the bottom and lay the short pieces of cardboard – 1 1/4″ x 6 1/8″ (3cm x 15.4cm) – up against the glued, short edges of the bottom. Lift up the Scotch tape strips and press them against the short sides of the box.

5. Make sure that the corners are well aligned and secure them with strips of Scotch tape.

6. Using a toothpick and working inside the box, spread some more strong glue around the edges.

7. Leave your box overnight to dry and the next day remove the Scotch tape carefully and sandpaper all the edges.

8. To give the bottom of your box a clean, professional look and to strengthen it, lay the bottom of the box on the sheet of thin cardboard, 6 1/2″ x 8 1/2″ (16cm x 21cm). Trace around the bottom of the box and cut out the rectangle. Spread glue all over the thin cardboard rectangle and glue it carefully into place, over the bottom of the box. Weigh it down lightly and leave it to dry.

III. Prepare the Plain Washi

You will now need the 1/4 sheet of plain washi. Working on the back of the washi sheet, measure and draw a rectangle 6 1/8" x 8 1/8" (15.4cm x 20.4cm). It is 1/16" (2mm) bigger on all sides than the bottom of the box. Cut off about 1/16" (2mm) diagonally from all four corners.

IV. Pasting I

1. Prepare your paste according to the instructions on the packet. Using either your finger or a brush that is 3/4" (2cm) wide, spread the paste onto the back of the washi rectangle. It is a good idea to spread the paste from the middle towards the outer edges. Let it sink in for a moment and brush off any excess paste.

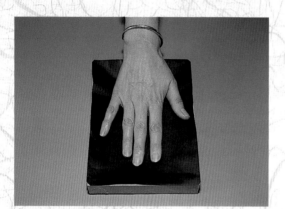

2. In order to place the washi lining right in the middle, I suggest you lay it first on top of the box edges and then press down with the palm of your hand.

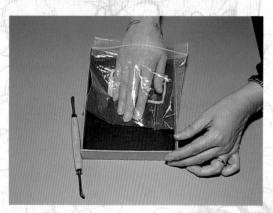

3. It is a good idea to put your hand in a plastic bag and use it like a glove to smooth the washi. Be careful not to use your nail or even to press too hard with the tip of your finger. Rub all over the surface to smooth out any air bubbles that might have been trapped under the washi when you pressed it down.

4. Then, using a blunt object, press along the edges and into the corners of the box. The washi lining is slightly larger than the actual size of the bottom of the box and so the washi will curl up the sides a little. Allow it to do that.

V. Patterned Washi

1. This is where your box starts to take on its final glory. Working with the patterned washi you have chosen, lay the box on the back side of the washi and trace around it.

2. You will need a border of 2 5/8" (6cm) all around, so measure and mark with a pencil several points 2 5/8" (6cm) from the traced line and join these points with a pencil and ruler.

3. Measure and make a pencil mark 2 5/8" (6cm) both horizontally and vertically from each corner of the border you've just drawn.

4. Now measure and make a second pencil mark 2" (5cm) from each corner, along the long edges only.

5. Using your ruler, draw a 2 5/8" (6cm) pencil line at 90 degrees to all the edges, beginning at the 2 5/8" (6cm) marks. That will be 8 lines. You should now have a square in each corner. Draw another 2 5/8" (6cm) line at 90 degrees from both ends of the long edges beginning at the 2" (5cm) mark to meet the 2 5/8" (6cm line).

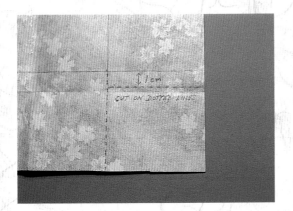

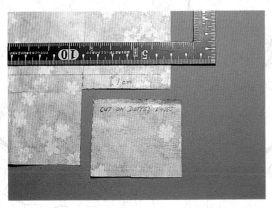

6. Cut along the dotted lines shown in the above photo. The approximately 1/2" (1cm) wide flap will be wrapped around the corner when you paste the washi around the box.

When you go on to make another box with different proportions, the following formula will, I hope, be useful:
1. Decide on the size of the bottom of the box.
2. 1 piece, the lid, should be 1/16" (2mm) bigger all round than the bottom.
3. 1 piece, the inner lid, should be 1/16" (2mm) smaller all round than the bottom.
4. 2 pieces should be as long as the long sides of the bottom and as wide as you wish the sides of the box to be high.
5. 2 pieces should be as long as the short sides of the bottom plus 1/8" (4mm) and as wide as you wish the sides of the box to be high.

VI. Pasting II

1. Spread the well-mixed paste all over the plain or back side of the washi. It is a good idea to spread the paste from the middle towards the outer edges. Wait a moment and then brush or wipe off any excess paste.

2. Set the bottom of the box onto the plain side of the washi, using the traced lines as a guide.

3. Pick up the box and washi, turn it over and, using either the side of your hand or a wad of cloth, smooth the surface of the washi.

4. Lift up the long sides first and paste them to the outer sides of the box. The small, 1/2″ long piece goes around the corner. Press the top of the 1/2″ (1cm) flap over and down into the box and at the same time fold the long sides of the washi down into the inside of the box too. The long sides overlap the small flap. If by chance the patterned washi is too long and curls across the bottom of the box, lift it up again carefully and quickly and cut it back so that it fits right into the inner edge of the box. Before the washi has time to dry on the inner sides of the box, press it against the inner sides and pay special attention to the inner edges. The back of a blunt knife or another blunt object will help to make a clean, sharp edge.

5. Fold over the short sides. I sometimes cut a 1/8″ (3mm) wedge off the ends of the short edges to reduce the bulk over the corners.

6. Go over all the edges with your fingers to be sure that the washi has been drawn tightly around the box.

7. Press into the inner corners with the blunt object to make them neat. I also use the sides of my pencil to go over the outside edges of the box to sharpen the contours. Again, smooth all surfaces and when you are satisfied that everything fits and is lying smoothly, put the box aside and leave it to dry.

VII. Lid

1. Lay the cardboard rectangle measuring 6 1/8″ x 8 1/8″ (15.4cm x 20.4cm) on the plain side of the patterned washi you have chosen and trace all around it. Lift off the cardboard and measure 1/2″ (1.5cm) at various points from the traced line. Join those points with a pencil. Cut along the outer line.

2. Measure 1″ (2.8cm) horizontally and vertically from each corner and mark those two points. Join each set of marks with a diagonal line. Cut along the lines across each corner. This will ensure tidy and non-bulky corners later on when you fold the corners. (See sketch on page 47, Flower Vase Chapter, Step IV "Make a Washi Pattern," Instruction 3.)

3. Spread some paste over the plain side of the washi and when it has had a moment to sink in, be sure to brush off any excess paste.

4. Lay the cardboard lid on the washi using the traced line as a guide.

5. Turn it over and smooth the surface with the side of your hand and your fingers. Fold over the long edges first and then the short ones. Using the tip of your thumb, press down the part of the cut that is nearest to the corner.

VIII. Inner lid

1. Using the plain, contrasting washi, repeat the steps described in part VII. The cardboard for the inner lid is 5 7/8″ x 7 7/8″ (14.6cm x 19.6cm).

2. Place the pieces separately either between towels or several layers of newspaper and weigh them down. I use a large wooden chopping block and then pile on as many heavy books as I can lay my hands on. Whether you use newspapers or towels, please change them from time to time until the cardboard is completely dry. This will take all day or overnight.

3. Glue the back sides of the lid and the inner lid together making sure that the borders are equal on all sides. I find it best to use clamps to hold the two parts of the lid together until the glue hardens. When the lids are wet with the glue, they tend to warp and it is hard to place them under something heavy without the one or the other lid slipping out of place. Allow it to dry.

IX. Finishing Touches

You might like to experiment by decorating the surface of your box with something small like buttons, shells or bows.

One easy and pretty idea is to cut out a piece of 1/16″ (2mm) thick cardboard 1 1/4″ (3.5cm) x 6″ (15.2cm). Cover it with plain, contrasting washi and glue it to one side of the top of your box.

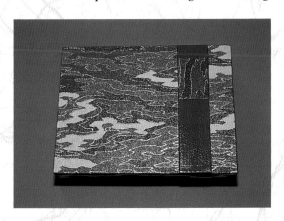

ASIA

JAPAN

Sakura Horikiri
1-25-3 Yanagibashi
Taito-ku, Tokyo
Tel: 03-3864-1773

Ito-ya
2-7-15 Ginza
Chuo-ku, Tokyo
Tel: 03-3561-8311

Origami Kaikan
1-7-14 Yushima
Bunkyo-ku, Tokyo
Tel: 03-3811-4025

Washikobo
1-8-10 Nishi-Azabu
Minato-ku, Tokyo
Tel: 03-3405-1841

Tokyu Hands
12-18 Udagawa-cho
Shibuya-ku, Tokyo
Tel: 03-5489-5111

NORTH AMERICA

USA

Mingei Int'l Museum
of World Folk Art
P.O. Box 553
4405 La Jolla Village
Drive
La Jolla, CA 92038
Tel: (619) 453-5300

H.G. Daniels Co.
(Artists Materials)
1844 India Street
San Diego, CA 92101
Tel: (619) 232-6601

Bunka-Do
340 East First Street
Los Angeles, CA 90012
Tel: (213) 625-1122

Elica's Paper
1801 Fourth Street
Berkeley, CA 94710
Tel: (510) 845-9530

Shizu
120 West Colorado
Boulevard
Pasadena, CA 91105
Tel: (626) 395-7293 or
(800) 248-0030
Fax: (626) 395-7290
(See also Internet infor-
mation)

Aiko's Art Materials
3347 N-Clark St.
Chicago, IL 60657
Tel: (312) 404-5600

Kate's Paperie
8 West 13th Street
New York, NY 10011
Tel: (212) 633-0570
&
561 Broadway
New York, NY 10012
Tel: (212) 941-9816

Zen Oriental Bookstore
521 Fifth Avenue
New York, NY 10017
Tel: (212) 697-0840

Uwajimaya
6th Avenue S. and S. King
Street
Seattle, WA 98104
Tel: (206) 624-6248
&
N.E. 24th and Bel-Red
Road
Bellevue, WA 98007
Tel: (206) 747-9012

CANADA

Japanese Paper Place
887 Queen Street, W.
Toronto, Ontario
Tel: (416) 369-0089

Shimizu Shoten Ltd.
349 East Hastings
Street
Vancouver, B.C.
Tel: (604) 689-3471

Little Japan
173 East Pender Street
Vancouver, B.C.
Tel: (604) 688-6255

EUROPE

FRANCE

Daimaru, France S.A.
Centre International de
Paris 55
2, place de la Porte
Maillot
75853 Paris Cédex 17
Tel: 40 68 21 05
Fax: 40 68 21 30

Junku (Japanese
Library)
18, rue des Pyramides
75001 Paris
Tel: 42 60 89 12
Fax: 49 27 04 84

Tokyo-do (Japanese
Library)
4-8, rue Sainte Anne
75001 Paris
Tel: 42 61 08 71
Fax: 42 86 90 24

GERMANY

Kyoto Porzellan GmbH
Immermann Str. 26
Düsseldorf
Tel: 0211-35 27 36

Tintenklecks
Papeteria
Bernd Plein
Gertruden Str. 33
50667 Cologne
Tel: 0221-2576063
Fax: 0221-2583361

UNITED KINGDOM

T.N. Lawrence
119 Clerkenwell Road,
London EC1R 5BY,
Tel: 071-242 3534

Paperchase Products Ltd
213 Tottenham Court
Road,
London W1P 9AF,
Tel: 071-580 8496

Falkiner Fine Papers
Ltd,
76 Southampton Row,
London WC1B 4AR,
Tel: 0171-831 1151
Fax:0171-430 1248

INTERNET

Shizu (orders taken for
delivery within North
America only):

http://www.shizu.com/
(homepage address)

info@shizu.com
(e-mail address)

If you need more advice
on where to find washi,
the author will be
pleased to assist you.
Please contact her direct-
ly at:

andrea.teddy
@t-online.de

For further information
on where washi is sold
near you, consult the
yellow pages and check
out the art supply stores
or handicraft shops in
your city. Another idea
is to ring the nearest
Japanese Chamber of
Commerce, Embassy or
Consulate and ask the
cultural department for
suggestions.